THE ELEMENTS OF SOCIAL JUSTICE

BY
L. T. HOBHOUSE

NEW YORK
HENRY HOLT AND COMPANY
1922

COPYRIGHT, 1922,
BY
HENRY HOLT AND COMPANY

172
H683e

Printed in U. S. A.

PREFACE

THE subject of this book is the social application of the ethical principles explained by the writer in *The Rational Good*. These principles are summarized in Chapter I so as to be intelligible without reference to the preceding work, to which the reader is referred for the fuller statement of the arguments on which they are based. The treatment as here developed is therefore in form deductive, but this is not to say that it is an attempt to apply abstract principles without experience. On the contrary, the only valid principles are those that emerge out of our experience, and the function of the highest generalizations is to knit our partial views together in a consistent whole. That our social philosophy must form such a whole and that our social efforts suffer from lack of articulate statement and rational coherence is only too palpable. To promote unity of aim among men of goodwill and lay a basis of co-operation between those attacking different sides of the social problem is a practical problem of the highest importance.

I have to thank Mr. J. A. Hobson for reading the MS., and suggesting many valuable emendations; and Mr. A. W. Perris for performing the same service with the proofs.

L. T. H.

WIMBLEDON,
   October 1, 1921.

CONTENTS

PAGE

CHAPTER I. ETHICS AND SOCIAL PHILOSOPHY. . . 3

Institutions are not ends but means. Politics are subordinate to Ethics. This was clearly recognised by the Utilitarians in insisting on the impartial application of the "Greatest Happiness principle." They erred in identifying happiness with pleasure and in the analysis of motive. The good as a harmony of Experience with Feeling. Harmony as opposed both to anarchy and repression. Harmony of attainment as the object of rational endeavour.

CHAPTER II. RIGHTS AND DUTIES. 22

On the principle of Harmony the Common Good cannot be opposed to the good of individuals, nor the rights of individuals set up against the Common Good as the doctrine of Natural Rights implied. A right imposes duties and is one term of a moral relation. It is not a condition precedent to social welfare but an element in social welfare. *Prima facie* conflict of rights. The test of operative consistency and the method of synthesis. Illustrated by the case of Nationality.

CHAPTER III. LIBERTY—(1) MORAL FREEDOM. . . 46

Freedom as self-determination in the absence of external constraint has an application beyond the life of man. Internally the life of a man is free as far as it is harmonious. Freedom of the will in the sense of indetermination is not ethically tenable. But implies determination by the outcome of action, and is not affected by the superficial externality of interests.

vi   *THE ELEMENTS OF SOCIAL JUSTICE*

CHAPTER IV. LIBERTY (*continued*).—(2) SOCIAL AND POLITICAL FREEDOM. 58

Freedom within a community involves restraints, in the form of a system of rights each of which is "a liberty." But what is the relation between "liberties" and liberty? Liberty rests on the spiritual character of personal and social development, and the protection of rights ("liberties") on the incompatibility in practice of opposed lines of conduct. In general no restraint is justified where no right is invaded. The extension and more complete definition of rights implies a better system of "liberties." This holds even of the extension of public rights so far as the State acts honestly and intelligently. For Liberty is the ground of Rights as such and as the central condition of development is a leading consideration in the definition of any given right. Tutelage of the immature and infirm mind is a duty, which must not be so interpreted as to impair the general principle of self-regulation. "Political liberty" is no adequate guarantee of personal freedom, but tends to secure government by the will prevalent in a community and thus to substitute the appeal to the will for force. Liberty in general as the replacement of Force by Will is both the effect and cause of social harmony. The historic development of Liberty and its present danger.

CHAPTER V. JUSTICE AND EQUALITY. 104

Equality, as an arguable principle of social organization, means absolute equality in some fundamental rights, or equal proportion of rights to desert, or to needs. These principles agree in founding the rights of the individual on personality. The equality of law consists in the universality of some fundamental rules and the impartial application of all rules. Justice involves an equal claim on the common good in respect of equal needs, subject to the adequate maintenance of necessary functions. Neither the development of one class at the expense of another, nor of the community at the expense of the individual can be justified by the principle of Harmony. The historical conflict between equality and inequality. Approximations to equality under physical limitations.

CHAPTER VI. PERSONAL JUSTICE. 138

Responsibility as the natural discipline of the will enforced by Retributive Justice which is founded on the harmonization of personal and common interests. This does not admit of the infliction of any evil for its own sake. Subdivisions of the treatment of justice.

CHAPTER VII. THE PAYMENT OF SERVICE. . . . 149

Exchange at equal market values is just only if values are determined on just principles. These involve the direction of the general economy to the provision of needs in proportion to their urgency, the non-existence of functionless wealth, the remuneration of all work required by the industrial system on terms adequate to maintain the worker's civic efficiency, and additional remuneration in proportion to increased vital costs. As long as the interest of the individual or the community are not fully harmonized by other methods remuneration should also increase in accordance with the social value of his work, in such wise that every field of work is on the whole equally attractive to ability. On this basis an economy resting on free exchange is ethically desirable.

CHAPTER VIII. PROPERTY AND ECONOMIC ORGANIZATION. 174

Property as the exclusive right of control. The attributes of property as such to be distinguished from those peculiar to private property. Property as the basis of freedom and of power. The assignment of property should be so conceived as to secure freedom for the individual and power for the community.

viii   THE ELEMENTS OF SOCIAL JUSTICE

PAGE

CHAPTER IX. SOCIAL AND PERSONAL FACTORS IN
WEALTH.   188

The claims of the community on wealth may be based on the performance of function, or on the absence of just claims on the part of any member. The position of inherited wealth. Social and unsocial wealth. Social and unsocial methods of gain. Resulting partition of ownership and direction as between the individual and the community. Cost and surplus the provision of needs.

CHAPTER X. INDUSTRIAL ORGANIZATION. . . .   206

When illegitimate elements of profit are excluded the direction of industry may sometimes be best conducted by private enterprise. Alternative methods of social control, by the State (or municipality), the Guild, or the co-operation of consumers. Whatever the executive direction the control of conditions of work must lie with an impartial body.

CHAPTER XI. DEMOCRACY.   217

The problem of democracy is how to secure any effective expression of will from the ordinary man. Majority rule is a necessary evil, tolerable as long as there is a real sense of community, but not when there are deep divisions as those of nationality. The difficulties are accentuated by conceptions of Sovereignty. Which is, further, incompatible with the ultimate unity of the human race. The functional theory of society valuable as suggesting cross divisions transcending territorial borders, subject to final co-ordination under a world league. The final authority not legal but spiritual.

INDEX.   245

THE ELEMENTS OF SOCIAL JUSTICE

CHAPTER I

ETHICS AND SOCIAL PHILOSOPHY

SOCIAL and political institutions are not ends in themselves. They are organs of social life, good or bad, according to the spirit which they embody. The social ideal is to be sought not in the faultless unchanging system of an institutional Utopia, but in the love of a spiritual life with its unfailing spring of harmonious growth unconfined. But growth has its conditions and the spiritual life its principles, the sum of which in the relation with which we are here concerned we call Social Justice. To define these conditions and display them as a consistent whole is the object of this book. In what institutions they may best be realized is a further question, on which history and psychology, economics and politics must have their say. We approach this problem towards the close of the volume, but our main concern is not with applications but with principles, not with institutions but with the ends that they serve. This is not a popular subject in political controversy, for it is obnoxious to those who, making success their god, naturally wish to discard all questions of right and wrong, and is hardly more attractive to the reformer, who sees a short cut to Utopia in some political or economic change in pursuit of which he is ready to

4   THE ELEMENTS OF SOCIAL JUSTICE

throw away everything that makes social life worth living. Both views are practically disastrous as they are theoretically false. Politics must be subordinate to Ethics,[1] and we must endeavour to see Ethics not in fragments but as a whole. The need of a reasoned ethical basis for political reform was more clearly recognized a hundred years ago than it is today, and perhaps that is one of the reasons why for a couple of generations the course of political improvement made steady strides, while the lack of such principles may

[1] It might have been expected that insubordination of politics to ethics, which is an integral part of Utilitarian doctrine, would have been taken up and insisted on by the Idealist critics of Benthamism. Unfortunately Idealistic thinkers in their very zeal for an ethical basis of society, tend to distort and even invert this relation. Bent on finding spiritual values in institutions, they come perilously near to justifying anything that exists, because it exists. They of course admit relative goodness and badness, but one of their ablest can write: "If we would avoid such scepticism about humanity as would paralyse all serious effort and make us hesitate to call anything right or wrong we must admit the fundamental rationality of all institutions and practical beliefs that have been able to hold their ground for some considerable time, and to afford shelter and supply cohesion to considerable numbers of human beings." Thus we must admit the fundamental rationality of slavery, serfdom, polygamy, polyandry, indissoluble marriage, divorce by mutual consent, animism, magic and witchcraft, polytheism, and also the denial of these beliefs. Why? Because "The evolution theory compels those who accept it to regard social cohesion and durability as the proof of some degree at least of ethical value and truth" (Ritchie, *Natural Rights,* pp. 16, 17). The evolution theory as such has nothing to do with ethical values, and if it compelled us to serve them so ill it would be self-condemned. What Professor Ritchie must have really meant is this: there must be some elements of goodness in or derivable from a society which maintains itself—not on the ground of the evolution theory

ETHICS AND SOCIAL PHILOSOPHY 5

partly explain why the forces of progress have fallen into disorder and left the world to the reign of violence. Whatever hostages it may have given to criticism, the Benthamite school had the merit of clearly and avowedly subordinating politics to ethics, and attempting to apply a simple and comprehensive theory of the good as the touchstone of all personal and social relations alike. The Greatest Happiness principle is now and long has been out of favour, but one of its most deter-

but of the nature of goodness as something that works socially. But it is one thing to say that there may be many good elements in a slave society and quite another to find slavery a rational institution. What is good may have survived in spite of slavery, and may have even turned some of the consequences of slavery (e.g. industrial organization) to good use (e.g. useful or artistic works). The social spirit of man which is good may turn to its own uses many of the products of the selfishness and fears and stupidities of man which are bad—and that is why the institutions which express these bad elements are so long preserved. The bad in society lives on the good. It may be added that there may be some good in an institution or some glimpse of truth in an idea which it would yet be absurd to describe as fundamentally rational. According to Mr. Cole (*Social Theory*, p. 15, etc.) social theory is not subordinate but complementary to Ethics, which he defines as the "theory of individual conduct" (p. 7). For me, Ethics is the theory of Ends or Values, whether realized in social relations or through individual conduct, and it is, I suppose, by the lack of such a theory of the disbelief in it that Mr. Cole is "driven back upon the individual consciousness and judgment as the basis of all social values" (p. 54). The aim of this book is to suggest an objective standard in place of individual, i.e. arbitrary choice, and the method is to lay down a theory of Ends which have been argued elsewhere and to deduce the principle of social organization therefrom. The "functions" which are the staple of Mr. Cole's theory can, as I think, only be valued, defined, limited and co-ordinated by the application of such principles.

mined critics, T. H. Green, recognized that it was as much for its virtues as for its vices that it was unpopular, and as I think that it contains valuable elements of truth that have been too much ignored, I propose to examine it here and sift if possible the grain from the chaff. Bentham's principle, then, is that actions are good in so far as they tend to promote the greatest possible happiness of the greatest possible number of those whom they affect. All questions of right and wrong were to be referred to this standard. What, for example, are the rights of property? Show that upon the whole private property tends to make the generality of people happy and you justify it. Show that it tends to make them unhappy and you condemn it. Show that any particular development of these rights has one or other of these effects and you justify it or condemn it, as the case may be. Show that in a given particular case the exercise of a right will cause misery though in general it is necessary to happiness, and you have then to consider the probable consequence of making exception. Now it may be, sometimes it clearly is, exceedingly difficult to make such calculations, but the principle has this element of value which the scientific sociologist may appreciate. It gives him an open field for investigation. He is tied by no rights or duties which are absolute and independent of all consequences. It is open to him to investigate freely all the conditions upon which human happiness and misery depend and from the best view that he can obtain draw his conclusions as to what is right and wrong in institutions. It does not by any means follow that he will put a low value on general rights and duties. On the contrary, a survey of society will probably convince him that one of the things generally necessary to human happiness is security, and that men can neither shape their own lives nor co-operate with one another unless they know what to expect and what is expected of them under given conditions, unless, that is, they have recognized rights and duties. At the same time he will see how important it is that rights and duties should be modifiable by a regular and agreed procedure in accordance with the changing requirements of human happiness. Thus the Utilitarian principle has at least the merit of providing a basis for an applied sociology.

Next, the principle, Hedonistic as it seems to be, possesses what some consider the austere merit and others the inhuman defect of a rigid impartiality. "Every one to count for one and nobody for more than one" is Bentham's rider to his formula.[1] "Between his own happiness and that of any other human being, the Utilitarian theory requires a man to be rigidly impartial," says J. S. Mill. A theory which carried this consequence is absurdly caricatured when it is stigmatized as a Pig-Philosophy. The question is rather whether it does not strain certain human virtues too far. Is it seriously contended that I am to care no more and do no more for my son's happiness than for that of any casual stranger? I am not quite sure what the orthodox reply would be, but I imagine that the Utilitarian would admit that par-

[1] "The happiness of the most helpless pauper constitutes as large a portion of the universal happiness as does that of the most powerful, most opulent member of the community" (*Constitutional Code*, I. xv. 7).

ental affection is one of the things generally necessary to social salvation and that the special rights and duties of the family play a beneficent part within the general circle of obligations. But he would go on to say, and here he would have right on his side, that the family feelings should not be a centre of collective selfishness but rather of radiant sympathy. They should enable me to understand and respect another man's feelings for his son, and only so will they work out in the end to the general happiness. In particular—here the essential doctrine of social equality strikes in—I must recognize that to all reasonable thinking the poor man's feeling for his son is much the same as the rich man's, the Jew's as the Gentile's, the bond as the free man's. In this respect, as in many others, men differ as individuals but not by classes. It is the relation itself and the depth, tenderness and purity of the affections involved in it that matter. The Utilitarian theory demands of us an equal recognition of human feelings of identical character wherever and in whomsoever found.

Criticism, however, has fastened mainly upon the term Happiness, and upon the Benthamite definition of the term. By Happiness, says Bentham, is intended Pleasure and the absence of Pain. Now this is so far true—and the element of truth is too rashly denied by critics—that Happiness is of the same generic nature as Pleasure. It is something that we feel and like to feel. Without feeling there would be no happiness. But Pleasure, both in ordinary language and in technical philosophic discussion, has generally meant a passing and partial condition, intense or languid as the case may be, but not depending for its intensity on any permanent conditions. The real value of life we feel to be deeper than this. We may feel a deep-seated unhappiness through the pleasure which is meant to distract us, and we may be sensible of an inward happiness triumphant over discomfort and pain. This happiness is not a matter of additions or subtractions, but rather of some stable relation in which we feel a profound and assured satisfaction. Perhaps we should rather say relations in plural, for there seem to be at least two conditions of such satisfaction. One is that we should be at peace with ourselves, for civil war is not a happy state. The other is that our life should be anchored in some object that takes us beyond ourselves, be that object another person, or our work, or the life of the community, or the God of our belief. To know what objects will permanently satisfy is to possess the secret of happiness, but for the moment the important point is that some object is essential, and the most serious criticism of Benthamism is that it seems to ignore the necessity. Regarding happiness as the whole and sole end, it depresses everything else to the status of a means. Now this does not consort with the psychology of happiness itself. We are happy in something, and the something must be worth while. Take from it its intrinsic value and our happiness becomes an illusion. If we are happy in things valuable only as a means to our happiness they would cease to be means to our happiness. What we wish for those we love is not merely that they should be happy on any terms, but also that they should be and do what we think worthy.

Their mistakes on this head involved the Benthamites

in a very paradoxical result. As a rule of life it is clear that the Utilitarian principle is altruistic—even, as has been said, austere in its altruism. It is an attempt to give precision to the command "Love thy neighbour as thyself." Yet the Benthamites became so entangled in questions of ends and means that their theory could be represented in the last resort as one of pure egoism. For when they faced the question of the motive appealing to the individual, they felt constrained to maintain that as happiness was the only good his own happiness must in the last resort be the good and the operating motive to the individual, the happiness of others being for him only a means thereto, or perhaps something incorporated with his own happiness by a process of association.[1]

[1] Any inconsistencies there may be in Bentham's various references to this question are amply explained by his autobiographical statement (*Works,* vol. x, p. 79-82), which to any one who can enter into the spirit of it, is a pathetic story of a philanthropist's disillusionment. The gist of it—it is, unfortunately, too long to quote—is that the "passion for improvement" which must be evident to every reader of his early *Fragment in Government,* is not likely to be extinguished but with life. Its "first embers" were kindled at the age of seven. "By an early pamphlet of Priestly . . . light was added to the warmth. In the phrase 'the greatest happiness of the greatest number' I then saw delineated for the first time a plan as well as a true standard for whatever is right or wrong, the useful, useless or mischievous in human conduct." Touchingly Bentham records his simple-minded certainty that he had only to publish what he had discovered and all the great and wise would fall in with it. "No sooner had my farthing candle been taken out of the bushel than I looked for the descent of torches to it from the highest regions"—those regions where as everyone assured him there dwelt nothing but goodwill. "Nothing could be more opposite to the truth. Instead of the universal sympathy, of which I had expected to see these graspings after improvement

ETHICS AND SOCIAL PHILOSOPHY

J. S. Mill made a step in advance by appealing to a fundamental social feeling whereby if it were properly developed the happiness of others might become identified with our own, but this does not meet the fundamental difficulty. For if, after all, on a collision arising I do actually feel that my happiness lies on one road and social happiness on another, which am I to choose? Is there or is there not a compelling obligation on me to choose the larger

productive in those higher regions, universal antipathy—antipathy on the part of all parties—was the result." There was "sympathy" only with his abilities based on the hope that they might be perverted. Bentham brooded, he tells us, till he was sixty, on the cause of these things, and not till that age did he discover the selfishness of mankind. "Now for some years past all inconsistencies, all surprises have vanished. . . . A clue to the interior of the labyrinth has been found; it is the principle of self-preference." Once found by this lovable, great, absurd, childlike nature it was, like all new—and embittering—discoveries, exaggerated. "Man from the very constitution of his nature prefers his own happiness to that of all other sensitive beings put together: but for this self-preference the species could not have had existence. . . . By this position neither the tenderest sympathy nor anything that commonly goes by the name of disinterestedness, improper and deceptive as the appellation is, is denied. Peregrinus Proteus, the man whom Lucian saw burning himself alive, though not altogether without reluctance, in the eyes of an admiring multitude and without any anticipation of a hereafter was no exception to it." For any pain or pleasure, however feeble, can under favourable circumstances swallow up all others, "as Aaron's serpent swallowed up all other serpents," and the pleasure of reputation had "obtained exclusive possession" of the mind of Proteus. In the same way, presumably, pleasure in the welfare of her child may swallow up every other pleasure in the mind of a mother, pleasure in the happiness of mankind every other pleasure in the mind of Bentham.

The interest of this passage is not logical but biographical. Bentham first, like many young people, thinks that everyone is and sink the smaller end, and is this obligation, if felt, rationally justified?[1]

To this question it was impossible to reply in the affirmative as long as action was attributed ultimately to desire and desire to an expectation of pleasure. But the relation of desire to pleasure was misconceived. When we desire something, not as a means to something else but as an end, we certainly anticipate pleasure in the attainment, but we do not think of the attainment as a mere means and the pleasure as a substantive end standing by itself and separable. If we did we should be quite prepared to sink the object of desire as soon as another means of obtaining equal pleasure is proposed. But this is precisely what in desiring and in proportion to the strength of desire we refuse to do. The advertisement says the baby "won't be happy till he gets it." It is useless for his mother to offer him something

---

filled with the same love of the kind with which he himself is brimming over. They only lack knowledge of the way of displaying it. Bentham shows them this way and is at once treated as an enemy of the people. He broods on the puzzle for forty years, and at last concludes that people love themselves most. This astounding discovery he generalizes into the principle of self-preference and at once is faced with the difficulty that after all many people—he himself to begin with—do not prefer themselves. This he gets out of by the mechanism of a disinterested pleasure without seeing that at bottom this is nothing but a verbal device wherein the substance of his self-preference principle is abandoned.

[1] To this Bentham, having accepted the self-preference principle, would clearly answer no. "When I say the greatest happiness of the whole community ought to be the end or object of pursuit . . . what is it that I express? this and no more, namely, that it is my wish, my desire, to see it taken for such. . . . (*Constitutional Code*, Introduction, § I. *Works*, ix, p. 4).

else which, as she quite well knows, might afford him equal satisfaction. As long as he is in the toils of desire he wants one thing and one thing only will satisfy him, and the mother, foiled in the attempt to satisfy desire with substitutes, has to undermine it by distracting attention and so starting afresh. It is the same in principle with the grown-up babies. A thinker is not satisfied till he has solved a problem. As long as he is in the grip of it nothing else appeals to him. It matters nothing that there are a dozen other problems that he might solve to his vast contentment. This does not ease desire. One of Mr. Shaw's characters gravely tells a young man that men of his age vastly exaggerate the difference between one young woman and another. It is possible that the young man might admit this with his intellect as a general truth holding in all cases but one. But it would be the exception that would still appeal to him, even though he should reach the stage of understanding that it would be much better for his happiness if it could be banished.

Desire, then, in its essence is an impulse not towards pleasure as such but towards some attainment as such. But at this point many critics of Utilitarianism have overstated their case. They have sought to reduce pleasure to the mere satisfaction of the impulse, the relief from the tension that keeps us on the stretch till the impulse is fulfilled. This is to ignore the difference between an agreeable and a disappointing result. Rosamond could not be happy without the purple jar, but possession showed her her mistake. Now there are many attractive things that disappoint us in the attainment, but in spite of the cynic there are many abiding or recurrent sources of satisfaction. Were it otherwise life would be nothing but a series of vain pursuits. In insisting on experience, on actual results in feeling, the Utilitarians were contending for the control of action by rational values as against mere animal instinct on the one side, or a vague and unchecked enthusiasm on the other. The truth is that something that we may call broadly feeling underlies desire from its inception to its fulfillment, prompting, controlling, and, in the end, if all goes well, confirming and approving. This last phase of feeling is not the least important in action, for it determines the future course of desire itself. As irrational beings we may continue to desire that which is only vapid or hateful when attained, but again in spite of the cynic, that is not the normal course of things. We see, then, in normal desire a certain harmony of feeling, action and experience. Feeling prompts and sustains a course of action arising in experiences which appeal to that very same feeling, and the feeling endeavours to maintain or renew the experience. The different elements concerned move in a circle, maintaining one another in activity, and it is this relation of mutual support which is intended by the term harmony. On the other hand, feeling and desire may fall asunder. Experience disappoints us and there is disharmony and frustration.

Now when we speak of anything whatever as good we are not making a merely intellectual proposition. We mean that it appeals to our feeling that we want to be it, to do it, to have it, to bring it about, to witness it, as the case may be. It is, in fact, something in harmony with our feeling, and here we see the root truth in the Utilitarian doctrine that the good is universally the Pleasurable. Conversely, if we really think a thing bad our feelings towards it are just the negation of the former. It is intrinsically displeasurable. The good, then, is a kind of harmony between feeling and action and experience. Unfortunately, what appeals to one spring of feeling in us as good may in itself, or perhaps in its consequences, appeal to some other strain of feeling as bad. What is to happen in such case we do not for the moment enquire, but it will be seen that, by our definition of the good as a harmony, it cannot be realized as long as there is strife between the feelings themselves. When we speak of a harmony between feeling and experience we must note that feeling is itself part of experience and the definition therefore includes a harmony between feeling and feeling. Again, unfortunately, what is one man's pleasure may be another's pain, so that there is a radical disharmony between two feelings though they are not feelings of the same individual. This quite bald opposition, however, can hold only if there is no sort of social relation between the two persons. If there is anything of the nature of Mill's social feeling within me there is a traitor in my camp, and the division between my neighbour and me is reflected in a division of my own feelings. These feelings, if given full scope and drawn out into all their consequences, compel me to include my neighbour, and with him in the end all men whom my action may affect, in the harmony that I can be satisfied with as really good, and to recognize any disharmony within this world of felt experience as evil; and this feeling, with all the burden of obligation that it carries, must be deemed reasonable. For in reason what we consider good as such we must hold to be good universally, and if it is good for me to prefer myself, then it is equally good for you to prefer yourself, and where our egoisms clash opposed actions will be equally good.[1] Reason as distinguished from feeling is not the basis of our social action, but the system of feeling at the basis of our social action is reasonable.[2] The fundamental principles in which this system of feeling expresses itself— e.g. that I must consider my neighbour as myself, are justified in reason, and the judgments of right and wrong founded upon them are true.

"Good" thus means a harmony of anything that in the widest sense may be called experience with feeling. "Experience" includes, besides that which is passively

---

[1] It may be urged that there is no absolute good, but that one thing is "good for me" and another good for you. This either means (a) that I can reasonably condemn you when you act in a way which is "bad for me." If so, however, I must also admit that you reasonably approve your own action. In that case, the same act is reasonably held good and bad by different people, and contradictory judgments about an act may, therefore, both be reasonable. Or (b) that I cannot condemn you because there is no "reasonable" good at all. This is equivalent to the admission that if there is anything which can be reasonably held good it must be universal in its application and not dependent on self or any partial preference.

[2] As the basis of action the Practical Reason is the harmonized body of impulse-feeling. As a standard or guide it is the order of life in which such a harmony can be expressed.

enjoyed or suffered, our actions and desires, and our feelings themselves, and it includes the experience in the same wide sense of all human beings. But in all relations there are endless collisions of feeling and only that can be reasonably and finally held good in which such collisions are overcome. This, it may be said, is to make the good an ideal unattainable by man, and such in a sense it is. But it will remain that everything that makes for the ideal is right, and every feeling and impulse that conflicts with it is wrong, for though there is stress and indeed disharmony in the very nature of the moral effort, the success of that effort is the way to a possible harmony while its failure involves a disharmony accepted as perpetual.

Nevertheless it cannot be too clearly understood that harmony is not the same thing as order resting on mere repression. We are apt to identify personal morality with self-control and good government with the maintenance of order. But in either case order resting on repression is not harmony. The impulse which is merely held down still subsists as a source of inner conflict. Possibly by persistent repression it may be extinguished, but contemporary psychology sees reason to think that even so it is either apt to emerge again in another form, or to become the centre of a deep-seated division operating below the threshold of our conscious life with ill effect psychological or physical. Still, it may be said, there are impulses with which we can make no compromise. Their satisfaction, to take our own criterion, is radically inconsistent with the main bent of our permanent feeling. Excise them and a harmony of the rest of our nature is possible. Admit them and no consistency can be reached. We cannot deny *a priori* that this is so. There may be radically bad impulses, original sin, and we may have to cut off a hand or a foot to enter the kingdom of heaven. That is, there may be within our own nature radical disharmonies which we have to accept as we accept what is untoward in external nature, our business being merely to minimize the ill effects as best we can. But this we can say, that if or in so far as an impulse can be so guided as to consist with the other requirements which we accept as necessary, then its repression is an unnecessary disharmony. There is a deep distinction between the repression of a fundamental impulse and the governance of the temporary desire in which such an impulse manifests itself. If something fundamental and ineradicable is persistently repressed, there is a permanent disharmony. Conversely, a harmonious personality develops in so far as the fundamental needs find satisfying expression in a consistent life. Just the same principles apply in social relations. It is possible, it is in fact necessary, to use a certain measure of repression in maintaining order, but in so far as that which is silenced is the voice of any real and persistent need of any class of men there remains a standing disharmony, and if this need could in fact be met without prejudice to the needs which are admitted it is an unnecessary disharmony and therefore wrong. Social like personal development will consist in finding more adequate expression for the fundamental needs not of some men but of all in a consistent working scheme.[1] In sum, repression as such is disharmony and is justified only so far as forced on us by something which we do not know how to work in with the partial harmony that we seek to preserve. Harmony is a plastic principle which does not destroy but remoulds.

The inner harmony of feeling and effort will be reflected as far as we control the conditions of nature in an outer harmony of attainment. In every gratified impulse we fulfil some part of our nature. If the fulfilment too often disappoints us it is because our nature is not in harmony with itself, and what is our gain is also our loss. It is this disharmony, supported perhaps by a fatalistic sense of the overwhelming power of the physical world, which has governed the pessimistic view of human achievement which has bidden us seek the good rather in renunciation than in achievement. But here we touch upon a contrast between the individual and the collective point of view. The individual may renounce all on his own account in order that he may better serve the good of mankind, but why should mankind as a whole renounce? Only it would seem for one of two reasons. One would be, that its aims and

[1] In this respect the Benthamite appeal to number is unsatisfactory. The happiness of many purchased at the expense of the few is better than that of the few purchased at the expense of the many. But it is not harmony. Harmony is not an algebraic sum with a positive result, but a pervading relation. It should, however, be noted that Bentham speaks of "the greatest happiness of all, or in the case of competition, the greatest happiness of the greatest number" (*Constitutional Code,* Introduction. *Works,* ix, p. 5).

interests are radically discrepant, which ceases to be true if a way of harmony is found. The other would be that, let men work together as they will, the way of nature is too hard for them, the major events of life, the ills that flesh is heir to, the death of those we love, the ultimate physical limitations on human progress, the "unscalable walls fixed with a word at the prime." To this the reply is that human power expands in self-accelerating measure, and that we can no longer fix the possible limits of the control of natural conditions by intelligence, provided always that the will to co-operate overcomes the dispersive forces. We do not yet know what man can make of human life when he sees it as a whole susceptible of a harmonious fulfilment. Through recorded history many good men have worked for many ends, most of them containing some good. But history is filled with their contentions. Suppose that the soul of goodness that was in them all could have understood its own meaning so that in place of internecine conflict there had been steady co-operation. It is not unreasonable to infer that under such conditions the world would have become a very different place from the world which we know. To forward this understanding is precisely the work of social philosophy. We set before ourselves a conception of the harmonious fulfilment of human capacity as the substance of happy life, and we have to enquire into the conditions of its realization. We consider laws, customs and institutions in respect of their functions not merely in maintaining any sort of social life, but in maintaining or promoting a harmonious life. The entire conception is, if you will, experimental, and the experiment that is to justify it must be made in practice. The value of theoretical discussion is in clearing up the conditions of success, in measuring results, in recognizing elements of success and failure, and planning necessary readjustments. The result must determine whether the thing can be done. But the experiment is worth the making.

CHAPTER II

RIGHTS AND DUTIES

As harmony has two opposites—repression and anarchy —so the social theory based on harmony has two opposites, a one-sided collectivism and a one-sided individualism. By a one-sided collectivism is intended the theory which conceives the life of the community as something qualitatively different from and superior to the lives of the component individuals. This opinion is supported by several plausible arguments which must be briefly noted.

To begin with, when *the* individual is contrasted with *the* community there is a half-suggestion that we are contrasting one man with millions, and assent is easily won to the proposition that the millions are the more important. The principle of harmony does not question that where interests are opposed the less must give way to the greater, and that on such occasions self-sacrifice is a duty, though it sees in the necessity of such sacrifice not a desirable austerity but a disharmony to be averted or overcome so far as the hard and cramping conditions of life allow. There is no essential dispute on this point. Further, it is true that any organized society may set before itself and may achieve ends which would be impracticable for its members if unorganized and perhaps would not appeal to them.[1] But according to our principle these must be ends which do appeal to the members of the community as members, and do further the fulfilment of their powers and the happiness of their lives as men and women. Those actions which have no such effect, such as national glory, power and territorial extension, are false aims for the community, precisely as in private life the corresponding ambitions are false aims for the individual. Again it is true that the community may rightly sacrifice something for the general benefit of civilization, or something of the good of all its present members for the good of their posterity. So precisely may an individual or a family make sacrifices for others, or postpone living to posthumous interests. In all cases the good, if it is real at all, is ultimately to be enjoyed by individuals. It is a harmony though presumably deemed a higher harmony, than that which the living temporarily forego—something which individuals ultimately share, not something to which they are permanently sacrificed.

And yet collective achievement does not always seem to make for personal happiness. Too often its very magnitude seems to crush or dwarf the individual. Indeed, it is easy to make a general indictment of the social tradition. In knowledge, it may be said, the enquiring mind is dulled and overwhelmed by erudition. In art imagination is fettered by academies. In industry organization involves a soul-destroying division of labour, and the civilized worker is the slave of a machine where the savage

---

[1] e.g. National defence, which of course can appeal to individuals only in proportion as they feel themselves united.

is a hunter or fisherman using his faculties as a whole. In politics "high" development involves a bureaucracy detached from the realities of life and ever grinding out Forms and Tables wherein men and women become units and percentages. A religion that begins as the spontaneous utterance of a soul grows into ecclesiasticism and a formulary. A principle of social progress for which its first apostles yield their all becomes the rote utterance of a party machine. Tradition preserves principles by canning them. Society may eke out life upon the tinned goods, but the vitamines are gone.

There is clearly a measure of truth in this indictment, but it does not establish any radical conflict between traditional acquirement and free vitality. If it did, our case would be hopeless, for we could make no permanent progress. What it really illustrates is the truism that partial and one-sided aims have their disadvantages, and things good in themselves are liable to misuse. Take the case of industry. By concentrating on mechanical invention and industrial organization, men vastly increased their wealth and their power over Nature. But in their eagerness they recked nothing of the effect on the producer. Is it surprising that they bequeathed a problem to the next generation? It is not what they achieved but what they neglected that caused the trouble. There is no reason to doubt that when we pay as much attention to the human side of labour as to the mechanical, we shall make of the new power a means of lightening the life of the worker no less than that of the owner. Take again the case of education. It is true that the weight of accumulated knowledge may become oppressive, and it is to be feared that most educational systems have a good deal to answer for in the way of exhausting the mind and stifling originality. But the reason is not that we have too much knowledge of things in general, but that we have too little knowledge of the art of education, or too little skill in applying it.

At any rate, of collective achievement as of collective aims, it holds good that its value is to be tested by its bearing on the actual lives of men and women.[1] What is sound in the collective life is that which completes the personal and carries it on to a higher harmony of wider sweep. What is unsound is that which, pretending superiority to the pettiness of personal life, is in reality moved by the pettier personal motives, such as those of ambition, egoism, love of domination and the rest, and by infusing these toxins into the spirit of community corrupts the best influences that might regenerate human life.

By reaction against the one-sided exaltation of the state we easily reach an equally one-sided individualism. This individualism may be defined as that which attributes to the individual as against society anything which really belongs to him only as a member of society. Outside the domain of theory this is a very common mode of thinking and speaking. Thus the successful man boasts of the great business which "I" have created without thought of the complex social engine which he found

---

[1] Strictly the Common Good is neither the sum of individual "goods" as independently determined, nor another kind of good opposed to them. It is the harmony of which each individual good is a constituent.

ready to hand. The poor man maintains "my" right to work and wages as though the community whose system of exchanges makes work profitable and gives money wages their value had nothing to say to the claim. The inheritor of wealth talks of "my" property, and resents interference with it by society, forgetting that without the organized force of the community and the rule of law, he could neither inherit nor be secure from moment to moment in his possession.

In social theory this one-sided individualism had its strongest expression in the doctrine of natural rights. The social character of duties has been generally recognized, but rights have often been attributed to the individual as though they were part of his skin, or one of his limbs. Without here attempting so much as a sketch of the history of the subject, it may be well to say a word as to the manner in which this opinion arose. "Right" is a conception of a reflective jurisprudence and "duty" of a reflective ethics. But there is a sense in which the rights and duties of individuals are defined and prescribed in every community from the simplest upwards. For the simplest communities that we know have a customary code in accordance with which a man knows under given conditions what he is to do and what he may expect, what woman he may court, whom he must avoid, what is his neighbour's property, what is common to the kindred or the community, to whom he should look as his protector or avenger, to whom he himself owes the obligation of support. There may be no regular organ for the enforcement of these obligations, yet they are recognized and habitually fulfilled. When they are broken the injured party may be left to self-redress, but in most cases self-redress has its rules prescribing the manner in which it should be carried out—whether by eye for eye and tooth for tooth or by exacting compensation—and the persons who should take part in it. These customs are accepted uncritically by each new generation as part of the very air that they breathe. If they require any theoretical backing, it is found in a vague sense of some misfortune that will ensue upon their breach, or in some more precise theory of a taboo, a curse, or finally the wrath of some spirit which transgression will excite. When communities become more organized and grow in extent through military power or enhanced wealth, they require a more definite machinery of government, and have to deal with a more complex situation, with serfs and slaves, or tributary peoples owning different customary codes. It becomes necessary to declare the law, and it is administered and enforced by courts. But what is declared is still deemed of sacred and inscrutable origin; it was delivered on Sinai; it is the law of the Medes and Persians which altereth not; it has not been changed since the days of Osiris; it "is not of to-day or yesterday, but lives for ever, and none knows whence it came." Yet it may press very unequally, and those who use it unscrupulously may grind the faces of the poor. Hence the magnificent protests of the Hebrew prophets, and eventually the legislation of Deuteronomy which characteristically is put forward as a version of the old law "found" in the Temple. Here we have the beginnings of protest and redress, but for systematic criticism we must await a self-governing people with a school of thinkers in their midst. In fifth-century Greece accordingly we find the variations and conventionalities of institutions exposed, and the whole fabric of law and government challenged as the artificial product of human agreement devoid of foundation in "nature." Plato undertook to meet this criticism by a systematic examination of the nature of man and the State, while Aristotle following him in fundamentals admitted a conventional element in legal justice, but insisted on a natural justice which has a certain validity everywhere because like the "natural" constitution it is the best. Aristotle thus touches, without elaborating, a conception of natural justice distinct from positive law. This conception became the centre of the Stoic teaching. Nature was the universal order animated and directed by God, to whose conditions all men had to conform. Apart from any positive institution, they were from first to last subject to the obligations which this system prescribed. But how were these obligations to be known? By this, primarily, that they are obligations holding of man as such, and therefore of all men as belonging not to "the city of Cecrops" but to "the city of Zeus," not as Romans, Greeks and barbarians, but as brothers and sons of God. Such universal truths might, it would seem, be found directly by asking what obligations seem axiomatic, e.g. the fulfilment of contracts, or negatively by considering what would remain if positive institutions were thought away. Hence in particular, restraints and inequalities being considered as creations of law, men were deemed "by nature" free and equal.

It is easy to see that the method concealed ambiguities,

and these have been so exhaustively exposed by a series of writers that they need not be examined here. Suffice it that in place of a reasoned statement of the ideal ends of society with which to compare the actual, the "Nature" which the Stoics and their long line of followers set up was a double-edged conception in which the notion of a simple and perfect rationality which might serve as the groundwork of ideal ends was blended with something supposedly real all the time and yet never actually realized, while the method of reaching it was by a series of abstractions which stripped social life of much of its wealth, and sometimes resulted in quite unreal and one-sided expressions.

Nevertheless the Law of Nature represented the first systematic attempt to conceive a rational system of law based on universal obligations, and claiming a higher authority than any institutions of State. As such it could be applied with beneficent effect by Stoic jurists in reforming Roman law, in humanizing slavery and sweeping away the archaic barbarities of the Roman family system. It could be applied in the seventeenth and eighteenth centuries as a check on tyranny, a plea for democracy, a method of overcoming international anarchy. It could be so used because, when all is said and done, it enshrined a real and profound truth. Locke is in the main right when he says: "The promises and bargains for truck, etc., between two men in Soldania, or between a Swiss and an Indian in the woods of America, are binding to them, though they are perfectly in a state of nature in reference to one another, for truth and keeping of faith belongs to man as man, and not as members of society."[1] He is right because the duty of keeping faith and the right of expecting it to be kept hold of men as soon as they enter into the relation of a bargain. They are not established by any political institutions, but are principles which every political organization must accept under penalty of disorganization if it ignores them. Criticism turns on the phase "State of nature," which as here used suggests that "by nature" men stand in casual temporary and external relations to one another. This is not what Locke really intends, for he conceives the state of nature as one in which men live sociably together without organized government. But the usage indicates the real logical danger of the term nature and the conception of social contract. For beginning with abstractions—the omission of elements from things as we know them—it is fatally easy to abstract too much, and in this case to skip clear from the subject of a civilized governance to the isolated individual in no social relations at all. When this is done, the individual is clothed with rights which are made to dominate instead of securing the common good, and are even divorced from duties because duties imply social ties.[2]

---

[1] *Second Treatise on Civil Government,* Book II, chap. ii.

[2] In his criticism of Locke, Green is right in so far as he has these points in view, but both historically and philosophically goes much further astray than the older philosopher in confusing the social with the political, and operative rules with enforced laws. When he says "a state of things out of which political society could have arisen by compact must have been one in which the individual regarded himself as a member of a society which has claims on him and on which he has claims, and such a society is

RIGHTS AND DUTIES

But a right, whatever else it may be, is one term of an obligation. It is something due to its owner, something therefore which imposes a constraint, whether by way of forbearance, acquiescence or active support, on other people. If a man has a right to a sum of money, this means that some one has the duty of paying it to him.

already in principle a political society" (*Principle*, p. 71) the shade of Locke may well retort that "in principle" is just as vague as "natural." Locke's point is that there may be social relations and even societies (and therefore among other things compacts) without organized government, and he correctly quotes the experience of American travellers in his support (chap. viii). When Green goes on that a society in which breach of obligation is not punished by a political superior is "not antecedent to political society but one which it gradually tends to produce" he is in conflict with facts of which Locke was partially aware and which were far more amply available to Green. When again Green admits that the State does not create rights, but "gives further reality to rights already existing" (p. 138) he admits the substance of Locke's contentions. I cannot here deal with Locke's whole theory of the Law of Nature, but I venture to register a protest against a school of critics who have done him much less than justice. Locke's view is both philosophically and anthropologically much nearer to the truth than that of Hobbes, Rousseau, Paine or any of the Hegelian school. I will only add that there is no clear thinking in these matters unless we distinguish (1) social relations which = human intercourse, (2) durable societies with a regular structure, (3) politically organized societies—states. Locke's point is that rights begin with (1), and this is profoundly true. There are rights and duties wherever there are social relations. There are recognized rights where there is a durable society though there be no political superior to enforce them and possibly not even a recognized means of enforcement. Even self-redress may have no regular rule (see my *Morals in Evolution,* chap. iii). There are crystallized and enforced rights when there is political society with a developed judiciary and police. In every case the moral right, recognized or not, is a claim which is a true element in the true common good of those affected (see below, pp. 35 ff).

If he has an exclusive right to a piece of property, this means that others must forbear from meddling with it without his leave. If he has the right to walk down the street, this means that no one must obstruct him. A right may not be recognized, but to recognize it is to admit an obligation in respect of it. Hence there is no sense in the proposition that in a state of nature a man has a right to do everything that he desired.[1] A man might claim everything, and so might his neighbour, but both could not have a right to dispose of the same thing according to their several wills. A right is, no doubt, a species of claim. What distinguishes it from other claims

[1] "Nature, say some of the interpreters of the pretended law of nature—nature gave to each man a right to everything, which is in effect but another way of saying, nature has given no such right to anybody; for in regard to most rights it is as true that what is every man's right is no man's right as that what is every man's business is no man's business" (Bentham, *Anarchical Fallacies; Works,* vol. ii, p. 502). In general for Bentham "natural rights is simple nonsense, natural and impresciptible rights rhetorical nonsense—nonsense upon stilts," or as he elsewhere says, "bawling upon paper" (pp. 494 and 501). In his *Constitutional Code,* however, Bentham can write "An original or primary right is that which is constituted by the absence of the correspondent obligation (i.e. it is something not forbidden). This is the sort of right which has place antecedently to the formation of government. . . . No man, as yet, being under any obligation to abstain from making use of anything, every man has, as yet, a right to make every use of everything" (*Constitutional Code,* I. iii; *Works,* vol. ix, p. 14). What Bentham here calls primary right is rather the negative side of right, i.e. the absence of an obligation to the contrary I have a right to do what I am not forbidden to do. That this is not the whole meaning of right is clear from Bentham's own remarks quoted above. If nothing is forbidden to anybody, and if a right is that which is not forbidden, then I have a right to this watch and you have a right to take it from me.

is that it is one which it is the duty of everyone to respect, and unless this distinction is admitted there is no reason for the use of the term, but all claims stand on the same moral footing. Thus right is a due seen from the point of view of the party to whom it is owed, and duty is the same thing seen from the point of view of the party owing it. Right involves a moral relation, and is not purely and simply the concern of the owner alone. The rights of men are not therefore conditions precedent to society, but move and have their being in social life.[1]

Neither are rights conditions precedent to social welfare, but elements in social welfare and deriving their authority

---

[1] One would like to say simply, "a right is one term of a social relation." But this does not seem wholly true of every right in every respect. A man is sometimes said not to do justice to his own emotions, or his own judgment, and I think the phrase is allowable. The implication is that there are elements within one which have rights as against other elements, and this is true if they have functions which it is good that they should perform as judged by their bearing on the personality as a whole. So I have a right to form my own opinion not merely as against others but as against my own fears and scruples. Apart from its social bearings, however, any such right has but a restricted sphere, for if others cannot inhibit my momentary thought or feeling they can arrest the expression in which it gains substance and momentum, and they may seek to worry and intimidate me until I am no longer master in my own mind. Further, if in fact I have a right to think for myself it is not a right peculiar to me, but one which I enjoy because it is well that men in general should so employ their faculties. The right has in fact often been challenged precisely on social grounds. In general terms a right is something due to an element in life as being for the good of the whole. This involves obligations in other elements. The individual man is an element in a social whole, and in general his rights impose obligations on other men. Thus the rights of man involve social relations.

therefrom. This is a direct inference from the principle of harmony which sees the good in a system of life shared by all who come into relation with one another, and deems anything that conflicts with such system bad and anything irrelevant to it indifferent. On this principle, then, any "right" which should in any way limit, hinder, or circumscribe the promotion of social welfare would be bad, and anything without bearing thereon would be indifferent. Such a "right" therefore would have no claim on our respect, which is a contradiction. Independently of the definition of the good as harmony, the same argument holds as long as we admit that we ought to do good and ought not to do what is bad or even that good or bad are what we desire to gain or avoid. For suppose any "right" to be such that not accidentally or through some passing conjecture of events but permanently and of its intrinsic nature its recognition would work evil to society at large, then a man has a right to demand, and it is other men's duty to do what inevitably works evil to mankind. At best such a principle could only be maintained by those who regard the good and evil of this life as of no account in comparison with the good or evil of some other life or some other mode of living, and even of these it may be said that judging by what they consider as real good and evil they still hold right—and also duty—subordinate to these conceptions. The contrast, however, once stated in these terms, is by no means academic, but involves the whole question of the meaning of human effort and human well-being. The question will not be pursued here. The reasons for conceiving human well-being upon this earth as a rational object of endeavour have been briefly indicated above, and I do not propose in this work to set them out more fully. It is enough for my purpose to point out that right and duty can only be set above the general well-being by a denial that the well-being of man on earth is the real aim of individual and collective effort.

It may be objected that both rights and duties do not occasion clash with public utility. A prescriptive right, say a right of property, may stand in the way of a public improvement. Does the right, then, *ipso facto,* disappear? The community has made a bargain which it proves inconvenient to carry out. Is the bargain null and void? If so, what becomes of the right? If not, how deny that rights govern public welfare? In general terms, the reply, of course, is that it is not in the long run for the public welfare that guarantees should be dishonoured. In general, it is necessary to the continuous working of social life that men should know what to expect under given conditions, and also what is expected of them. The contention is simply that the rights assured to them and the duties demanded of them should be such as upon the whole conform most closely to the conditions of the common welfare. In anything but a perfect order occasions will arise in which strict adherence to these conditions will involve society in some loss. But this is a small matter compared with the violation of one of the permanent conditions of social co-operation.

Rights and duties, then, are conditions of social welfare, or as we define such welfare, of a life of harmony. A general rule of right or duty is one in general necessary to social welfare. A particular right or duty is that which in a given case, all things considered, is necessary to social welfare. To this welfare, then, every member of the community stands in a double relation. He has his share in it. That is the sum of his rights. He has to contribute his share. That is the sum of his duties. Rights and duties thus rest on the same ethical foundation. The fulfilment of each personality is a constituent element of the common good, and the individual may justly claim the conditions necessary to it, the forbearance of others, and their aid in so far as the general conditions of the community allow. A man's right, speaking generally, is a claim upon others which he may make or which may be made for him, and which is maintained by some impartial standard.[1] A legal right is a claim recog-

[1] Compare Ritchie, *Natural Rights*, p. 78. The definition which Professor Ritchie there quotes from Professor Holland, "one man's capacity of influencing the actions of another by means not of his own strength but of the opinion or force of society" is surely too narrow. A baby has rights, an imbecile has rights, and I see no real objection to saying that an animal has rights. Green's contention that only a "person" has rights (*Principles*, p. 46, etc.) rests on his conviction that real good resides only in the moral will. Those who, like myself, find good and evil in the whole world of feeling and its related behaviour from the merest sentience upwards, naturally take a different view. But a baby has of itself no capacity to influence the actions, say, of the trustees of its estate. What is more serious, a man may have a right which society does not recognize, so that it gives him no capacity to influence anybody.

It may be objected that this proves too much, since a baby cannot make a claim. Others, however, can make the claim for it, and yet the claim is still the baby's. Even a recognized right, then, is not the owner's capacity to influence, but some one's capacity to influence. Further, a right may be so little recognized that even the owner makes no claim, but to hold it a true right

RIGHTS AND DUTIES 37

nized by law, a recognized moral right is a claim which the actual moral judgment of the community upholds. A true moral right is one which is demonstrably justifiable by relation to the common good, whether it is actually recognized or not. On the other hand, the individual has no moral rights which conflict with the common good,[1] as therein every rational aim is included and harmonized. It is true in a sense that rights of the individual are founded on personality. They are the conditions of personal development. But personality is itself an ele-

---

is to deem it something which he might or even ought to claim. With this understanding I think the definition in the text may stand.

What is most important in this matter is to be clear on the question of recognition. Green's dictum (*Political Oblig.* p. 140) that there is no right, but thinking makes it so, must be set aside as inconsistent with his own better teaching. Professor Ritchie (loc. cit.) appears to follow Green, defining a moral right as a claim recognized by Society, but in the course of his discussion he comes to recognize rights as determined by the good of society (see e.g. pp. 101, *et seq.*). The objection to his account is that he slurs the converse truth that the good of society is bound up with the recognition of the rights of its members.

[1] This is not by any means to say that he is without rights against the community, for the community may misjudge the common good. Green (op. cit. p. 110) says "a right against society, in distinction from a right to be treated as a member of society, is a contradiction in terms." If this means "as a member of society ought to be treated" it is true enough. If it means "as a member of this or that community with such rights as the community chooses to assign to its members" it is profoundly wrong. We British blandly tell the Irish that they are members of our society, offer proof in clearest Black-and-Tan of the meaning of this privilege, and then through our most high-souled politicians lecture the Irish on the innate criminality which is forever prompting their resistance to our brotherly law.

ment in the common good, and that is why its rights have moral validity. In general terms, a true right is an element in or condition of the real welfare of its possessor, which on the principle of harmony is an integral part of the common welfare.

So far we have personal rights in mind. But we may usefully generalize the conception. Any constituent element that is necessary to the life of the community may be said to have its rights. Thus any corporate personality—a family, a municipality, a company, a trade union is a possible subject of rights. We may even say that functions, or at any rate, the representatives of functions have their rights. Thus religion, patriotism, education, in so far as they contribute to the common good, have a function to perform and a certain claim on society to maintain the conditions under which those functions are best fulfilled. In fact, if those conditions are not maintained they are starved, and the common life is so far the poorer. Finally, the community itself may be said to have rights, that is just claims upon its members and all its constituent elements.[1] Putting these points together, we may say that an acknowledged right supposes a community in which conduct is organized with a view to a common good. It is something claimed by and due to an element in the community, or to the community as a whole from its elements.

[1] Such claims in strictness need an impartial tribunal to determine them. In fact, the interpretation of legal rights is so effected. Where there is a written constitution the same principle limits legislation. Otherwise through the legislature the community defines its own rights. We are not to assume that it **always does** so in the spirit of an impartial court.

Distinct rights and duties are based on distinct elements of the common welfare. If accurately determined, they must accordingly form a harmonious system. But this condition is not easily fulfilled. No one can pretend to know accurately all the conditions of the common welfare in all circumstances. The consequence is that rights and duties, as we understand them, may come into conflict with one another. For a given rule may state correctly enough what is required in one relation, that is to say, what would be our right or our duty in view of that relation alone, and another rule may state no less truly what would be required in view of another condition or another relation alone. Unfortunately, the various relations of life do not lie side by side, but are intermixed so that rules founded on any one of them may conflict with rules founded on another. For instance, I ought to observe a compact and I ought not to injure an innocent person in any of his legitimate interests. But what is to happen if by some unforeseen consequence a compact that I have made with A operates to compel me to inflict such an injury on B? There are two opposed fallacies to be avoided. The first is the fallacy of erecting certain rules into absolute principles. This is in general to make one relation of life dominate all others, which is to put the part above the whole. It may be urged that there are some conditions of welfare which are universal in their application, i.e. condition all relations of life alike. If that is so it must be rejoined that they are not easy to formulate unless in such very abstract terms as give very little help in practice. The one supreme rule is the right of the common welfare as such. But to recognize this is to make straight the way for the opposite fallacy which suggests that all rights being subservient to the common welfare this should be the test in any particular case. What need of general rules? Consider what will work out best here and now, under the given conditions. This is the rule of expediency to which we have already referred. The case against it is that it ignores the important truths that the permanent welfare of humanity rests on definite conditions, that people cannot live from hand to mouth, but need security and certainty in their mutual relations as the basis of any fruitful co-operation. As a fact, in one way or another, by a combination of influences that need not be analysed here, rules have arisen prescribing the duties and assigning the rights that arise in given relations or on given conditions—rules that appear just and reasonable in each relation, having in view that relation alone. It is clear that on the principle of harmony, or indeed on any rational principle, we must go on to ask how these various rules consist with one another, and when we do not find consistency we must readjust, and must continue our readjustment until we have a system in which all the parts work together. Each of the parts as thus remodelled will give us one of the conditions of the general harmony, and will, therefore, be a true and rational rule of right or duty, as the case may be. To set it aside, then, is to violate a condition of the common good.[1] On the other

---

[1] Professor Ritchie writes, "Science must have no prejudices and therefore we must admit that there was a stage in human development when slavery, being useful to the progress of mankind, was not contrary to what could then have been considered

RIGHTS AND DUTIES

hand, to take a "right" without such criticism as absolute may be to violate every other condition of the common good. Rights and duties, then, are not conditions limiting the common good from without, but conditions constituting the common good in the varying situations of life and the intermingled relations of men.

The violation of any rule of right which has stood the critical test is therefore a violation of some condition of the common welfare. However convenient it may be for some immediate purpose, such violation must on the hypothesis work harm. It must, all things considered, be a net loss, and, as a violation of a system which depends as a whole on its consistent operation, the loss is not to be measured in quantitative terms. It is an injury to the spirit of the common life. The over-riding of a *prima facie* right is another matter. It may be the mere

'Natural Rights,' although when slavery is no longer an institution of progressive societies, it becomes contrary to what people now consider 'Natural Rights'" (op. cit. p. 104). People who so begin thinking of Rights will soon take the more logical step of banishing once for all a term which has ceased to give any guidance. Whether at any stage useful or not, a slave system violates essential conditions of harmony. This is not a truth dependent on conditions of time and place, but plainly legible in the history of slave states themselves. Slavery may have displaced other disharmonies which were even worse, and its products may have been used by the better elements in the social system for ends good in themselves. Neither of these possibilities cancels our first proposition.

On the tendency of Professor Ritchie's entire treatment to "the annihilation of all individual rights even regarded as derivative," see Mr. J. A. Hobson, *The Social Problem,* p. 94. T. H. Green, in whom we get most of the cream of Idealism and least of its sour milk, writes: "The essential thing in political society is a power which guarantees men's rights" (*Political Obligations,* p. 102).

correction of an error. It may be a synthesis in which we are dealing with two or more claims founded on several aspects of the case. Either claim would very likely be right if its particular aspect stood alone, but the true right of the concrete case must be founded on both aspects together, and the synthesis awards to each "aspect" what is its due *in this relation*. A compromise falls short of a synthesis. At its best it maintains the more important elements of each claim considered, but gives up something which belongs to the true right *in the case*. At its worst it merely aims at securing agreement—or the appearance of it—by mutual concession.

Abstract as all this sounds, it merely formulates the working rule of the best statesmanship. The most difficult problems of politics arise when a claim based on solid and substantial grounds clashes with another claim no less solid and substantial in itself. In such cases the statesman shows his wisdom by a synthesis in which the substance of each claim is preserved but its spirit transformed by relation to the common good; the politician shows his cleverness by a compromise in which enough is given to each claimant to keep him quiet without reference to the permanent effect on the common welfare; the strong man shows his weakness by shutting the door on inconvenient facts, and feigning to have done with them; and the fanatic shows his temper by standing on the last letter of his claim. Theory cannot provide the statesman *a priori* with rules for effecting his synthesis. What it can say in justification of his method is (*a*) that every valid claim of right rests on some real condition of the common good; (*b*) that this cannot be established till all relevant

RIGHTS AND DUTIES 43

conditions have been compared, and that until this is done the use of the term "right" is question-begging; (c) that if in the settlement any real condition of the common good is violated, there remains a disharmony which will operate in fact, however its manifestations may be repressed; (d) that owing to the interdependence of elements in social life this disharmony is likely to spread and invade other conditions of harmony.

Let us by way of illustration take the difficult claim of nationality. Let us for the sake of argument assume the general rights of democracy and government by free discussion between all parties concerned. Let us finally assume the rough definition of nationality as the claim of a people united by certain ties of sentiment and tradition to form a distinctive and united community. This claim, then, rests as Mill argued, on the desire of those concerned, and if we grant that the desires of the governed are to determine the nature of the government we must *prima facie* accept the claim. But (a) the people in question may include among them minorities who have opposed desires, and (b) their desire for separation may conflict with some valid claim of other people with whom they are at present associated. It may be, for example, that the nationality which desires independence holds territory which is the strategic or economic key to the state of which they at present form a part. There is no *a priori* right of nationality, which lays down that a people so circumstanced should be given a kind of monopoly or unqualified power to use their advantageous position for their own ends. Nor again, in relation to minorities, is there any *a priori* method of determining where the process of division and subdivision should end—whether with six counties or four or one or with part of a county, or finally, with villages, streets or individual houses. The practical statesman moves in accordance with pure ethical theory when he insists on examining such a position as a whole, endeavouring to discover those real conditions of harmonious co-operation under which each rival claim would be transmuted into a spirit of loyal contribution to a common cause. If any of these claims is founded on real conditions, if, e.g, the national sentiment rests on deep-seated and reasonable grounds, it may be ignored and its protests suppressed, but it is not thereby expunged from reality. Driven under, it propagates a disharmony which eventually invades the wider and more elementary conditions of the democratic principle involving the prohibition of free speech, arbitrary arrest, picked juries, and finally martial law, reprisals, arson and murder. The unacknowledged right takes its revenge by undermining the rights which deemed themselves secure.

Rights and duties, then, are determined by the contribution which they make to the harmony of life as a whole. That determination is effected in general terms by the application of ethical principles to the summed experience of the race. The resulting system may seem to savour of the abstract and the Utopian. It would be truer to say that it is one that can only be reached by a highly developed community, for it is from the experience of the highly developed communities that it is drawn. But with their experience it stands in close relation, being formed by the selection of what does actually operate harmoniously in their lives, and the rejection of the disharmonious. Finally, to all progressive statesmanship, to all wise guidance of any people at whatever stage, the general principle of harmony propounds a very simple and comprehensive rule. Deal with the disharmony which faces you. He who removes one cause of conflict without exciting another opens a new opportunity without closing an old one, lifts the weight of a repression without weakening respect for law, enlarges the scope of harmony however far he may be from realizing all its conditions. What is from one point of view the remote goal of social endeavour is more adequately conceived as a principle actually operating in every stage of human life, expanding or contracting in response to efforts wisely and justly conceived or selfishly and foolishly directed.

CHAPTER III

LIBERTY

(1) Moral Freedom

MAN, said Rousseau, is born free, but is everywhere in chains. It would be nearer the truth to say, "Man is born in chains but is everywhere struggling to be free." Everywhere, that is to say, where the human spirit has vitality. Where it is not born, or has died, men accept the chains. The sign of life is the renewal of the struggle to emerge from controls or conditions that curb and cramp. Yet over and over again the escape seems illusory, and men emancipate themselves from one form of control to pass under another. They can obtain freedom from this or that control, they can obtain freedom in this or that respect. But whether they can attain freedom in general, whether freedom unqualified is a coherent ideal, is not so easy to say. Nor is it at first sight clear why men desire freedom perhaps above all other things. For freedom seems a negative condition, and men are not satisfied with negations. Freedom may be said to involve power or, at lowest, opportunity. But of opportunity we may make good use or bad, and it is only the good use that seems to be a positive element in our well-being. Perhaps there is

LIBERTY

one element of illusion in our desire for freedom—the illusion of unlimited potentiality. Let us but escape from the superincumbent weight of government, of the church, of the social order, of any particular obligations—and I will show you what I can do! The sense of indefinite repressed powers that seem all the greater because we have not tried them, dazzles us with visions, magnified by the haze, of the life that we might live if only the obstruction were lifted. Life so seen is richer and more generously endowed than life as it really is in proportion as the possible is larger than the actual. But though there is an element of illusion in the love of freedom, there is a solid core which it is essential to understand. We must try to discover what freedom means—in what sense it is attainable for man in society, and what part it plays in the social welfare.

Moral, social and political freedom is the property of rational beings,[1] but it is worth noticing that the term freedom has a wider and it would seem quite legitimate use. The unbandaged limb is set free. The muscle when the tendon is out is free to contract, the blood is driven through the narrow arteries and tiny capillaries, but moves "freely" when it reaches the larger veins. A pendulum swings freely from its support, a wheel revolves freely in a vertical plane about its axis, and an arrangement being made by which the axis is free to revolve vertically, the wheel then moves "freely" in three dimensions. Energy is "liberated" when some

[1] i.e. of man with some doubtful reservations in favour of the higher animals. These raise questions of interest in themselves but not essential to the present purpose.

check or tension is cancelled. A body from which the support is withdrawn falls "freely" to the ground. The point clearly common to all these cases is the removal of some restraint, or some external impelling force. External constraint is the antithesis of liberty, and the most obvious definition of the term is absence of such constraint. In the case of things physical, however, it is easily seen that their absence is never complete. For example, the limb may be set free from the bandage, but its movements then pass under the control of the nervous system, and if set "free" from these by amputation it dies. The wheel is free to revolve, but what sets it revolving? The body is "free" to fall, but it is not free to remain suspended in mid air. There is another party to the question, a predominant partner, the earth. A physical body may be free from something specified, or in some respect, but it experiences more swiftly, regularly and completely that which we saw that man has often to learn—that to escape from one control is to pass under another. Yet if we look carefully we find certain differences among the controlling conditions which, to a limit, distinguish the free from the constrained body. A watch will not go without the aid of the purely external force which winds it up. But once wound up it marks the time for so many hours in virtue of the mutual tensions and pressures of a cunningly contrived system of parts. Each one of these parts moves by push or pull of another, but if the mechanism as a whole goes, as we say, I think, with perfect propriety "of itself," that is its condition, and its motions at any moment are the continuation of the condition and motions of the previous moment, and are in short their effect. Given the winding up, the watch as a going concern is internally determined. It is true that the watch remains subject to external conditions and that some of these, e.g. temperature, may affect its time-keeping, and it is true that in the physical universe such subjection can never vanish. But it may vary very greatly in importance from place to place, and it varies inversely to the importance of the internal factors. There seems nothing to prevent us from describing a mechanical system as working "freely" in so far as its operations are the total result of internal factors, and as "constrained" in so far as its operations depend on external factors. We thus arrive even in the physical world at a positive conception of freedom which precisely matches the negative. Freedom is determination by internal factors and the absence of constraint from without. Such freedom would be absolute or complete only in a system which could be isolated from the universe, or in the physical universe itself as a whole if unaffected by anything not physical. In other cases, freedom is partial or relative. It is freedom from some particular constraint, or exercisable in some particular respect.

The freedom which man seeks is similarly an escape from constraint which enables him to live in accordance with the impulses of which he is sensible within himself. He may be constrained by physical barriers, by a disease—which though part of his body is an external oppressor for his "self"—by his master or lord, by his neighbours, by the pressure of circumstances, by his own engagements. These "constrain" him in so far as they obstruct his self-determination, that is to say, the operation of the internal factors and his effective demand for freedom is generally for the removal of some specific restraint acutely felt as such an obstruction. But what is the freedom of man within? What are the internal factors which are to determine him? Notoriously they are various and conflicting, and the freedom of one may be the constraint or destruction of another. A man may be set free from all external restraint only to find himself the slave of a passion. From such slavery ordinary morals tell us that he is to be set free by his will. The will would be free internally if it had mastered all else, but would the man necessarily be free? It is possible that the will itself may be both a hard task-master and a slave—a hard master in repressing spontaneous springs of life and feeling, a slave in rigid adherence to some maxim imposed on it by suggestion that by no means expresses its whole nature. Or we may put it, granted that the will may obtain freedom by perfect mastery, is the will the man, or is the man the whole internal system of thoughts, emotions, imaginings, impulses, conscious and unconscious? We have seen that these various elements may conflict and cannot, therefore, all be entirely free, but is there any sense in which the whole which they constitute can be free as a whole, or must freedom be the prerogative of some governing part such as the will by which the rest is subdued? The reply is that there is freedom just as far as there is harmony. Any one element may contribute to the consecutive actions and interests of the man, and so far as it does so is acting "of itself" and unconstrained. There is no theoretical reason why this harmony should not extend to the whole of a man's nature, and in fact it is that peculiarity which throws man in strongest contrast to the physical world; that while the parts of a watch remain what they are made and work well or ill as they were made, the elements of human nature show an indefinite degree of adaptability to one another and to the requirements of the whole. Hence, if perfect harmony is like all other perfection an ideal, it is an ideal to which approximation is always possible. It is clear from the nature of harmony that such approximation cannot be effected through the sheer repression of impulse or emotion by will. Repression is the opposite of harmony. It has a necessary function, but true harmony is effected by a subtler process in which the root impulses, checked in their crude manifestations, come to adapt themselves to the permanent requirements of life and find their satisfaction therein, while the "will," that is the self in its active unity, finds itself not opposed but fortified in its power and enlarged in its scope by their contribution. Life is thus unified not by repression but by harmony, and so far as this principle extends it is, internally regarded, free as a whole.

Popular discussions of free will turn more often on the conception of choice than of internal determination. Indeed, they seem to assume that determination of any kind is the contradiction of freedom. The will, it is thought, must be free in the sense that it stands like an arbiter above every prompting of impulse or solicitation and gives a decision which up to the very momoment when it is put in force it may—again without solicitation—revoke. If this last point is pressed a further requirement comes into view. The will may change abruptly and, above all, without cause or reason. If it is not (as our account has suggested) a system of interacting elements or the principle of harmony among such elements, neither is it a simple substance of permanent character, nor again a being of changing character, but so changing as to follow out an evolution of its own. Either of these three descriptions might be taken as formulating different cases of "self-determination." For e.g. a simple, unchanging substance may be said to determine itself in the sense that its existence at this moment is the cause of its existence in the time immediately following, and the same would hold of a complex system whose successive phases thus emerge out of one another, or a simple being which evolves (if that be possible) by a law of its own. But any of these views alike offends the theory now under consideration. For it, the will must be free not only of external influences—whether outer objects or impulses within the self—but of its own past. Its course of development, so to say, may sweep continuously onward to such and such a point and at that point may be completely broken. This break (of which *prima facie* examples may be given) is not to be explained (as the analysis of those examples will generally suggest) by any "cause." No new experience, no special suggestion, not even the brimming-over of forces that have been accumulating— no such expression will at all suit the case. The will decides, and there is the beginning and the end. For this view then the freedom of the will does not mean either determination by internal factors or mastery of anything and everything outside itself. It does not mean either self-determination or absence of present restraints. It means essentially freedom from the past—its own past included. The will is cause but never effect. It brings events about but is not itself brought about—not even by its own previous being. Essentially, it is a new being every time it acts.

This view is generally combated on the strength of the universality of causation. But the principle of causation may itself be called in question, and to examine it would lead me beyond my purpose. It is sufficient here to say: (1) that in vindicating the freedom of the will the so-called Libertarian principle destroys that which it proposes to liberate. *The* will disappears when its continuity is broken. It is replaced by so many separate volitional acts, "free" like beads scattered sparsely on a string, that neither pull nor push one another, but move or rest each "of itself." The "I" which wills this now has nothing to say to the "I" of yesterday or of five minutes hence. Each choice is a new fact arising out of the void and plunging into it again. There is no will which abides, whether changeless or growing by successive acts of self-determination, for there is no self-determination. (2) The two arguments by which the Libertarian theory supports itself may be turned against it. The first is the argument from Responsibility. It is held that I cannot be responsible for my acts if they grow out of my past, and my past ultimately out of my ancestry and my circumstances. It must be replied that I cannot be held responsible unless I am the same agent that did the deed. If the doer was a will which popped up out of nothing, it was not the "I" of this moment whom you accuse, but the fleeting disconnected "I" of *that* moment, which you should blame. The "I" of this moment is free and might take a quite contrary line. Responsibility implies continued self-determination.

The second argument is the appeal to direct introspection. Look into yourself and you are aware at any moment that within the limits of physical possibility you are free to choose this or that. Your past does not bind you. No propounded motive binds you. The choice is yours. To this we may reply: "Quite so, you are aware of your own self-determination, that the choice is the output of your own being as it is then and there constituted. You are aware among other things that no past decision constrains you, that no past precedent finally fetters you, that you may adopt any new suggestion and for that matter think out for yourself and follow any new plan even while the hour is striking. In this sense you are conscious of freedom from the past. But to be aware of the non-existence of your own continuity is a different thing. You may not indeed be fully aware of all the threads that connect your being. Some of them lie deep in the unconscious, and no introspection is sufficient evidence of their presence or possible evidence of their absence. But that consciousness on the whole testifies to persistence is evidenced by its use of the term 'I,' which if it means anything means the identical being that was and is through a period of time. In its use of the term, consciousness implies that I have become what I am."

Yet there is one relation in which in deliberate, purposive will I am in a sense free of my past. In planning I think forward. I see things as they bear on the future, consider them in their causal character as engendering effects or tending so to do. In willing I adopt some end as my purpse, and in the same way I act or move forwards. The causal tendency of my act is the reason of its performance. I do it for what it tends to bring about and the act of choice itself is that organization of the internal factors which tends to the effect. Thus I do not act because of the past but because of the future, and it is this which does "free" me from a purely mechanical sequence in which each detail follows the past, without varying in relation to the consequences which will proceed in turn from itself. The past, including all that I have been, has made me what at this moment I am—in that sense I am never free of it—but what I am is a being with face set to the future, determined in action by the causal tendency of the action itself, free therefore from that mechanical determination by the past in which future consequences have no share. This, which is in germ the character of all conation, comes to mature and clear expression in deliberate will. But my will is after all predictable? By anyone who knows its character accurately, knows how it values things, knows how it will bring new elements into synthesis and what the law of any purposive, creative synthesis must be, yes. To anyone who proceeds by taking successive points in the evolution of the will and linking them up so as to form a curve of development, no. That method will not suit a thing so constituted as to be guided at any moment by the operative tendency of its own act at that moment. If we could forecast the whole spiritual life of mind it would be only by appreciating the content of fully developed spiritual ends with all their values and the conditions under which they might be realized. We should have to begin by knowing the end and work backwards. We could not reach the end as we do a mechanical result by starting from the original constellation of forces and working forwards.

Moral freedom, we conclude, means self-determination in the sense defined. It involves continuity in the self, and is therefore incompatible with conceptions of freedom which require in each act of choice a breach with the past. But it also involves a determination by the causal tendency of the factors involved which prohibits any prediction from the facts of the past without resting on a knowledge of the values to the realization of which the mind looks forward. We have yet to ask how far such internal freedom is realizable by a being who lives in a world of which he has a part and has few, if any, "values" or objects which are not referent to this world. We have spoken of impulses, promptings, motives. What are motives but external objects in one shape or form—things or persons as they are or as they may be? If these things act on my will how can it determine itself? If they do not act on it, what is the will to do in the resulting vacuum?

LIBERTY

The answer to these questions is familiar, and may be given very briefly here. The object in reference to which I act, though in itself external to me, makes its appeal to me through susceptibilities and interests which are a part of me. My love of A, my jealousy of B, my hunger and thirst, my coldness or warmth dispose me to the modes of action which I pursue to A or B or food or drink, to the fire or the open window. All that I do in relation to both is the expression of something that is within me. True, the first stir of prompting comes from without, but if it met with no response within there the matter would end. Sometimes indeed the object seems to tyrannize. "The steel itself drags the man on." "The woman tempted me and I did eat." But it was the traitor within the gates of self that must bear the blame, or if there are obsession and tyranny, still there must be some impulse or emotion within that tyrannizes. Conversely, I am "free" from all such tyranny if my self as a whole is master in its own house, lord, or, better, leader of all its constituent emotions, interests, impulses. Moral freedom, then, has nothing to do with isolation, but is, as has been said, the harmony of the whole self in the multitudinous external relations which constitute the web of its interest.

CHAPTER IV

LIBERTY (*Continued*)

SOCIAL AND POLITICAL FREEDOM

THE moral freedom of man, then, is proportionate to internal harmony of a being who is guided by impulses and feelings turning upon ends mainly external to himself. What now of the freedom of man in society? When many men live together can they be free? If one can do what he will he may if he chooses put any sort of constraint upon another. If, on the other hand, he is restrained from so doing he in turn seems not to be free. James I meant by a "free monarchy" a system in which the king was responsible to no one. In such a system one man would be free but nobody else, and this is not a system which anyone except the one would call free. What then is meant by freedom in social life or by a free community?

There is one very obvious sense in which a community may be called free, viz. in the sense that it is independent of any other community. As to this sort of freedom more will be said later, but it will be well to deal first with freedom within the community. Now a man is most obviously unfree when he is in the power of another, and he most obviously becomes free when emancipated from such power. But does anyone (even our free monarch) ever really cease to be dependent on others? Are we not all bound by law and government, by our position, by the obligations we have assumed, and so on, and are we not thus compelled to be guided more or less completely, as the case may be, by the will of others? These are points which we must examine, but let us at once remark that there is a distinction between arbitrary power and regular power. It is one thing to be bound by law and subject to its interpreters and administrators, and another to be at the mercy of individual caprice. It is at least the first step in freedom to be emancipated from the arbitrary power of the individual, even if we only exchange it for the uniform and impartial control of law.[1] Some thinkers would seem to consider this first step to be also the last step and to conceive a Utopia of comprehensive regulations in which certainly no man could tryannize or exploit another because no one could move outside the narrowly prescribed path. If this does not satisfy our conception of a free life we must look further. It is not sufficient that law should protect us from arbitrary power. It is neces-

[1] The implication is that the control of law is impersonal and based on the common good. Unfortunately, laws must be interpreted and administered by individuals, and where there is much regulation the householder may find himself dependent for the simplest comforts or even necessaries on the majesty of law as represented by the judgment of some fifth-rate Jack-in-office. Law fails to emancipate from the control of the individual in proportion as it leaves latitude of interpretation to its ministers. Hence, advocates of liberty have generally demanded rigid definition, yet rigidity may cut with terrible harshness into real needs of individual cases and then the cry is for elasticity. This is the inevitable dilemma of legal regulation.

sary that law, customs and institutions should themselves be free, that is compatible with freedom of life for those who live under their shadow. How can this be? What freedom can the members of a community in general enjoy except by relaxation of order, and does not relaxation of order if pushed far enough allow the unregulated powers of individuals (or even the blind tyranny of circumstances) to reassert themselves, while at the least it is the sacrifice of one good thing for the sake of another?

A community as a collective whole and all its members as individuals in close inter-action might be absolutely free if their natures were absolutely harmonious, just as the individual man might be free internally if all the elements within him harmonized. This, however, could only be possible by a miracle of pre-established harmony, which miracle the Disposer of things has not performed. We may, however, say that a society is in fact free in proportion as its internal life is harmonious. Just in that proportion all constraint drops away and goodwill and ready service take its place. But in so far as men's natures are out of harmony restraints are required. They are required by freedom as much as by harmony, for, as already remarked, the uncharted freedom of one would be the unconditional servitude of all but that one, and conversely a freedom to be enjoyed by all must impose some restraint upon all. If I am free to do this, take that, or go this way, that means that neither you nor anyone else must prevent me. The respect in which I am free places a limiting restraint upon everyone else. The guaranteed system of liberities is, therefore, the obverse of an enforceable system of restraints.[1]

If Liberty involves restraint, it may be asked whether its pursuit is not illusory. What is gained from the point of view of liberty by substituting one system of restraints for another? Can we find one system of restraints which is consistent with liberty, while others are inconsistent? To this question one answer that has been given is that, from the point of view of liberty, the restraint required may be expressed in the formula "to every man full liberty, provided that he does not interfere with the like liberty of another." This restraint, it is contended, is a restraint conceived wholly and solely in the interest of liberty itself, and consists merely in generalizing or socializing the Liberty Principle. It is designed to meet precisely the objection to absolute liberty which we have noted, and secures to all as much liberty as is compatible with a life in common, that is, as much as can be shared by all members of a community. But it is clear that, literally interpreted, this principle is not compatible with social order, nor even with liberty itself. The liberty of A to knock down B is not

[1] "Liberty as against the coercion of the law may, it is true, be given . . . by the simple repeal of the coercing law. But as against the coercion applicable by individual to individual no liberty can be given to one man but in proportion as it is taken from another. All coercive laws therefore . . . and in particular all laws creative of liberty are, as far as they go, abrogative of liberty" (Bentham, *Anarchical Fallacies; Works,* vol. ii, p. 503). Yet how many people professing and calling themselves Benthamites have opposed legislation intended to check the abuse of power by individuals in the name of Liberty and the supposed Benthamite individualism.

sufficiently confined by the corresponding liberty of B to knock down A, if he can. If A is a trained pugilist, while B is an ordinary man, A might use his liberty to extort what he would, and B would be in his power. With no essential modification, the same argument will apply to any means of coercion that one man may exert upon another. The right of the weaker party to use similar means, if he happened to possess them, is a very poor consolation to him for the absence of real and present protection. It is evident that what the weaker party needs is, not the right to retaliate, but security in the enjoyment of the rights which he possesses, and if rights are founded on real conditions of well-being, it is for the common good that this security should be given him. Whatever happens to liberty then, it must respect the acknowledged rights of all members of the community.

A doctrine which comes closer to this view is that which draws a distinction between self-regarding acts and those which affect other people. Yet, on the principle of the common good, it is clear that there can be no purely self-regarding actions strictly so called, and if there were, that they still would not stand outside the region of common concern. In the first place, it is difficult to assert of any act that it has no effect upon others whatever. Not only have example and contagion to be taken into account, but the mere effect upon the individual himself has a social aspect. His functions as a member of the community may be improved or impaired by any part of his conduct. But in the second place, even were there acts which could affect the indvidual alone, they could not be socially indifferent. The good of each is, on the principle of the common good, matter of concern to all. Thus, though there be actions which are directly and predominantly self-regarding, this is not in itself a sufficient justification for leaving them to the free choice of the agent. Liberty is not founded on the personal right of the individual as opposed to, or as limiting the right of the community. But though there is nothing good or evil to the individual which can remain indifferent to the community, it does not follow that the good is to be sought or the evil averted by compulsion, and the question which is before us at present, is on what conditions compulsion is required. How far compulsion may be applied to a man for his own good we may consider later, but we may begin by drawing a distinction between acts which do and acts which do not invade the rights of others. This invasion may be by way of force or fraud, but it also may be more indirect. Thus, without violating any acknowledged right, a man may use his power to secure the consent of another to terms incompatible with the general conditions of his well-being, and the State may be compelled, for this reason, to regulate contracts between parties of unequal economic strength. Again, by merely exercising their right to deal exclusively with one another, certain parties might drive a common enemy out of the arena of competition. In general, the use of any sort of power, whether directly or indirectly, to encroach upon the rights of a member of the community, may require restraint just as much as overt force or detected fraud. It is upon the nature of such undue advantage and the means of limiting it that a great deal of the modern controversy with regard to the limits of liberty, on the one hand, and State control on the other, has turned. Yet there should be here no controversy of principle. If it is once admitted that the community should protect each of its members in the enjoyment of certain rights, as conditions of well-being, the method by which those rights are being impugned is of secondary importance. If for a moment the infringement appears to arise from the legitimate pursuit of a right, the reflection must follow that such pursuit cannot, under the circumstances, be legitimate, and that what is needed is a closer definition of the right relied upon, so that it can no longer be used in a manner adverse to some general condition of well-being.

The liberty of each then must, on the principle of the common good, be limited by the rights of all. But this restriction is less hostile to liberty than at first sight might appear, for under normal circumstances every right is a liberty. It is security in the enjoyment of something which I can use as I will. The right of personal protection, for example, gives me liberty as against the interference of any capricious person to do what I will with my own limbs and my own body. My rights of property give me the free disposal, precisely so far as the right is unqualified, over material objects. The rights of conscience, of discussion, of expression, of public meeting, of religious worship, are so many powers which I may or may not use, as I think fit. Thus, in general, my rights are my liberties, and in protecting my rights, the community secures my liberties, while conversely, if it permits or commits infringement of my rights, to that extent it permits or commits infringement of my liberties. Thus, in the body of rights, we have found a system of restraints which is the basis of a system of liberties.

So far we have confined ourselves to the rights of individuals, but the community as a whole has its interests. The individual owes it his service as a duty; how far can it demand that service as a right? That is to say, where there is a difference of opinion, in which we must give to both sides the credit of bona fides, what right has the community, acting through its established organ, the Government, to impose its will upon a recusant minority? We must assume, for the moment, that the Government acts honestly, according to its lights. Now, it may be able to secure the common objects without compulsion. If so, there seems no adequate reason why it should constrain any unwilling member, and coercion, as involving a disharmony, appears wrong. On the other hand, the common purpose may be such that, unless all contribute to it, it will fail. The very essence of a rule may be that it should be observed by all without exception, and it is, in fact, on this ground that the community exerts its authority in the protection of individuals. But whatever the object may be, let us suppose that it is one judged necessary to the common well-being and to depend upon universal acquiescence. If this acquiescence is refused, it appears to be the right of the community to enforce it—a right justified by the requirements of the common good as judged, not indeed infallibly, but by the best available lights.

The formula that liberty is limited by rights requires, then, the addendum that rights must include, in addition to the rights of individual members, the right of the community as a whole. We thus arrive at the conception of a system of rights which are also liberties, while if liberty is limited only by rights there will, in addition, be a more general liberty of doing anything which does not invade any specific rights. Within these limits, it may be suggested, each individual is free to act in accordance with his own judgment and at his own will. To this account it may be objected firstly that it is indeterminate, and secondly that it involves a vicious circle. It is indeterminate because rights rest on conditions of the common welfare which must in large measure be matters of opinion. The lack of a final and conclusive judgment on this point is precisely one of the grounds on which liberty of thought and action is claimed, and it seems futile accordingly to construct a definition of liberty which throws us back on the problematical and unknown. Further, the definition, even if true, involves (it may be said) a circle because liberty itself is claimed as a condition of well-being and therefore as a right. As to the first point, let us for the moment make no assumption of any finality in the determination of rights, but let it be granted that at any rate a claim of right expresses the will of somebody and that though there are many wishes without basis in right, there is no prima facie claim of right without a basis in will. Transferring the problem to this ground we then observe that the ends willed by A may or may not clash with the ends willed by B. If they do not clash, if A and B are able to pursue each his own ends, then the meaning of our principle is that mere dislike of A's proceedings, or the belief that they are bad for him, does not justify B in attempting to suppress them. This is the meaning intended by the "general" liberty of our definition, and it holds even if in the place of B we write "the community." If, on the other hand, A's ends and B's cannot be reconciled, a different question arises. We have now to think not only of their respective wills, characters, opinions, etc., but of the results in which these issue, and, as these results are incompatible, we have to choose between them. There cannot from the nature of the case be liberty for both. The choice ought to rest on the best judgment that we can make of the bearing of either end on the common welfare. That is the meaning of the more specific part of our principle. Whichever end is supported by the common welfare is a "right," which sets a limit to any liberty that might encroach upon it, while itself carrying the liberty to pursue it. It is at this point that our second difficulty arises. Liberty itself, or some kind of liberty, may be an essential element in the common welfare. If that is so it will not do to define it in negative terms as that which does not interfere with other rights. It requires a positive definition as that which itself will not be interfered with. The question is the more important because if liberty as such is a right it must affect our valuation of rights in general. Wherever there is a conflict there must be some restriction of liberty, but other things equal it will always be the lesser liberty that we shall exclude.

Two questions are then raised. The first is, why it should be wrong to suppress by force or intimidation a type of will character or opinion merely as such a type of will character or opinion. To answer this is to get at the heart of liberty, and thus to prepare for the second question, viz. what part liberty is to play in determining the very rights by which its sphere is defined. The character and opinions of each man are integral to his "good." The good of each individual is a part of the common good. Why, then, should there be any element in it to be left entirely to his judgment? Suppose his judgment unsound, so that he seeks the bad or the less good? He does not, it may be, interfere with the rest of us in the pursuit of our ends, but are we to pass by on the other side? Must we not interfere with him for his good (as a part of the common good)? This is not to assume infallibility.[1] Our judgment is fallible

---

[1] We claim infallibility on any point only when we regard the question as closed. We claim general infallibility only when we cease to regard opportunities of discussion and experiment as intrinsically necessary for higher development. From this point of view to draw a distinction between the expression of opinion on the one hand and action on the other is important. The dissentients may express their feelings and seek to convince us, provided that by their acts they do not prevent us from doing what we judge necessary. It is true that the line between expression of opinion and incitement to action is not always easy to draw with precision. That is a necessary hindrance to the close application of the principle, but it does not destroy the principle itself. The greatest possible freedom of speech, writing and meeting may be made compatible with a rigid insistence on public order. In the same category with speech fall actions that do not invade any right. A congregation may worship God in its own way without preventing others from following their own mode of religion. If

LIBERTY

as his is, but this is the limitation under which all human purposes are pursued. We must form the best judgment that we can of what is good and then act on it. Otherwise we cannot act at all. If this is granted, why should we not coerce a man for his own good?

Again, if we consider social purposes, are there any that are in fact unaffected by the recalcitrance of individuals? Consider religious worship and belief. It may be said that any number of people are free to form themselves into a church, to organize instruction among themselves, and to pursue that form of worship which they think right and best. They are not let and hindered in so doing by the abstention of others. Admitting this,

it is urged, as in the text, that the craving for universal conformity may be a part of a religion, this is a desire that, on a true interpretation of the spiritual order, must be set aside. It is precisely in a spiritual order that external conformity without inner agreement is a delusion. A community possessed of the religious conviction that it is its duty to compel all men to conform is doubtless on its own principles justified in doing so. But its principles may reasonably be discarded as wrong by the spiritual interpretation of the Common Good, and not only as wrong but if the foundation principles of the religion are spiritual, as internally inconsistent. To put it more generally, religious worship is rightly left free so long as it invades no rights. Religious acts, e.g. human sacrifice which do invade rights, are rightly prohibited on that ground.

It may be urged that ethically one religion is superior to another, and that those who hold this view should seek to suppress what they regard as a centre of corruption. But the reply is that they should do so by rational means, by the appeal to reason and feeling. The problem set to the rational good by the conditions of its own nature is that of securing acceptance by proving its superiority, and of making its way in the minds of men by the constraint of the mind and not by coercion.

they may still object that the full efficacy of their religious life is impaired by the non-conformity of the rest of the world. They cannot realize the particular kind of social development which is their ideal. They desire, for example, a world-wide communion, and a part of the world will not come into their communion. May they not go out into the highways and hedges and compel them to come in? The mere existence of centres of disagreement is injurious to the full self-confidence of faith. Will not faith be exalted by destroying them? In general, may it not be a condition of the Common Good as conceived by the best lights available that every one should be made to conform to the same pattern of conduct in action, in word, and as far as possible in thought, so that all centres of resistance to the best teaching may be destroyed? If so, there is at once no place for any kind of liberty outside the ruling creed.

Both these problems point to a deeper basis for the doctrine of liberty than that balance of rights which we have contemplated. Liberty rests on the spiritual nature of the social bond, and on the rational character of the Common Good. Consider first the good of the individual. We find this on our principles in some form of personal development. What form is no doubt a large question. But its peculiar difficulties do not really arise here. The point for us is simply that there is no enduring good for the individual except in the fulfilment of his personality. Now when a man overcomes a bad impulse by his own sense of right and wrong his will asserts itself, and it is by such assertions of the will that personality is developed. If by the action of others he

LIBERTY

is persuaded or stimulated to an act of self-control, if conduct is set before him in a new light, if wider bearings of action are seen, or dormant feelings evoked—in all these cases his working conception of the good is extended or defined. But where he is merely coerced no such development takes place. On the contrary, so far as coercion extends there is a certain moral pauperization, the exertion of will is rendered unnecessary and is atrophied. The same reasoning applies if it is a question rather of what we call judgment than of will. If a man is simply told what he must or must not do his judgment is at best unaffected, while if his whole life is thus guarded without reference to his own thought and feeling it is atrophied. It follows that it is only by action on a man's reason and feelings that his good is to be sought, and thus that it is only through this rational or spiritual medium that the Common Good is to flourish. In so far in short as the Common Good consists in the things of the mind it can thrive only through the conditions of mental growth, through the interchange of ideas, the contagion of emotion, the spiritual unity which exists only for those who themselves experience it. Compulsion is only deemed necessary to secure the predominance of a creed by those who do not in their hearts believe that creed to be strong enough to avail by its own acceptability. Lastly a spiritual order involves mutual forbearance as well as mutual aid—the exercise of this forbearance is a desirable feature in the social personality. The capacity to tolerate divergence and overleap differences in the sense of a profounder identity is the condition of the highest harmony in an imperfect society.

Personal development is spiritual or rational in that it consists in the extension of the sphere of experience dominated by governing conceptions which tend to organize thought, feeling and action into a whole. We call such a growth spiritual because in it the psychical elements are not cut into shape with the knife, but are transfused with the spirit or meaning of the whole. This is the nature of development in a social personality, and the development of society as a whole is the same in kind. There is no such growth in the mere suppression or elimination of a type or opinion. There is growth when an antagonistic element is so modified by being brought into relation to a higher or wider conception as to find not merely tolerance but an active function within it—for example, when the gift of freedom makes a rebellious people into loyal subjects. There is growth through the war of interests when they are subsumed under a higher conception of unity. There is no growth where unity can only maintain itself by keeping rival interests down without seeking to find their legitimate sphere. Thus, even if we had achieved finality in the theory of life we should have to lead men up to it through freedom rather than bend them to conformity by coercion. But if we are far from finality and all of us alike have to learn, freedom becomes a necessity not merely for individual but for collective progress. It is a question of laying ourselves open to illumination and to criticism from every possible quarter. This does not mean that we are to go without any rule until we have found the perfect rule. It means that we must hold our rules subject to revision and amendment. In our practical and our theoretic interests the rational procedure is essentially the same. The function of reason is to harmonize experience. It is not for reason to dictate on the strength of its own *a priori* conception what experience there can be. It is its function to take experience and the primary judgments founded on experience and weave them into a whole, rejecting in them only that which upon trial it cannot reduce to consistency. The first principle in conducting this process is, that no experience can be left out and no inference from or judgment formed upon experience rejected or modified except on the ground of a demonstrated inconsistency which it would introduce into the order of thought. Now in practical matters, as individuals differ, so do their experiences and their interpretations of experiences. Each different personality is then a separate medium of truth. Precisely in proportion to his divergence from the normal a man may contribute something fresh to the common stock. His line of divergence may be such that what he contributes turns out to be poor and false. But this is to be judged by its demonstrated incoherence. That is, it is to be judged by reason. To suppress it unheard is to abdicate the function of reason as the impulse to co-ordinate all possible data. The sphere of reason grows not by the eliminations of data but by the extension of unifying conceptions over a wider field of more heterogeneous data.

Nor does the case of opinion differ in this relation from that of action. The difference is between that which obstructs, defeats, frustrates others and that which does not. But in itself we may regard the line of action to which each individual is prompted by his interpretation of his experience as supplying data for the synthesis to be affected by rational conceptions. This synthesis expands and deepens in proportion as it absorbs fresh elements, and so makes possible a wider life and a fuller harmony of divergent personalities. Just as the individual personality attains its fulfilment by a harmony of inner development, so the Common Good develops by a wider and more complex harmony resting on the unconstrained, that is the rational, interaction of mind and mind. The harmony of the inner development is the unit of the social harmony.

As conditions of harmony then we contemplate two very different kinds of constraint. In the one a man is constrained by conviction. He comes to realize his true good not in some course dictated by self-will but in a modification of that course which opens to him a life compatible with and contributing to the life of society. In the other there is no such regeneration or reconstitution of the rebellious individual. He is coerced[1] but not convinced, his personality is thwarted, and no modified

---

[1] Whether coercion is applied by law or public opinion is quite indifferent in this connection. Coercion means either (1) deterrence by pain or threat, which merely suppresses impulse without occasioning either change of heart or enlargement of view, but rather tending to obstruct any such improvement. Or (2) it means the literal prevention of an act, as by the physical restriction of liberty or by making it impossible. Thus a Trade Union can compel agreement to its terms by making the alternative impossible. The agency by which coercion is applied is not material in this connection.

line of development is found for it to pursue. The case is in essentials the same with the impulses of the individual in relation to his own will. The impulse may be merely inhibited, or it may be reconstituted so that what is fundamentally the same impulse which threatened to wreck his personality may be reconciled with his scheme of life and made to serve it. In the one case there is development, in the other merely arrest; in the one rational constraint, in the other what we call coercion. The resort to coercion blocks the more secure road to harmony through the sense of uncompelled allegiance. At the same time it pauperizes the reason itself by requiring it to surrender its work to force.

The ultimate foundation of liberty, then, is that it is a condition of spiritual growth. The price we pay for it is that so far as a man is free to do right he is also free to do wrong. He cannot be free to make the best of himself without also being free to reject the best, and those who seem to suggest the contrary are, I fear, trying to get the best of two incompatible worlds. We may make a man conform outwardly to what we consider the best standard or we can let him decide for himself. But we cannot at once leave the decision to him and be certain that he will conform.[1] Now when

---

[1] Positive or real liberty, says Professor Ritchie (*Natural Rights,* p. 139) "means the opportunity or capacity of doing something. Such liberty is, in its turn, good or bad according as the things which can be done are good or bad." This precisely omits the vital point of liberty. It is good that man should exercise his own will. The good loses one-half of its goodness if not done from choice, and if there is choice there must be the chance that the good will be rejected.

a man does wrong it is useless to pretend that it is a matter of no social concern. If we do not prevent him by physical compulsion or the threat of punishment, it is because we think the remedy worse than the disease. But if this is so, what place remains for coercive restraint? Have we not proved too much, and must we not, to be consistent, allow a universal and unchartered freedom, trusting that men may learn by their mistakes to act rationally? The reply is that this is to ignore the effects of the mistakes or crimes of A on the fortunes of B and C and the community at large. Let us, as above, without making any initial assumption as to which is right or who is wrong, merely put the case that the aims of A are incompatible with those of B. Both cannot have their way. Which are we to support? There is no question here of liberty in general against restraint in general, but of one liberty against another or one restraint against another. We can find an impartial principle of decision only if we can specify some condition of the common welfare which A violates and to which B's requirement conforms. This we express by saying that B is within his rights and A is violating them. We may, of course, be wrong in our judgment of the conditions of the common welfare, but if we have done our best according to our lights to ascertain it correctly, then we owe it to B and to ourselves as a community to maintain this condition unimpaired. We are not seeking to convert A by restraining him, but to save B and the common weal.

Thus we seek to prevent the invasion of any right whether by force, fraud, or the use of advantage, because rights are as we judge conditions essential to the general well-being. But, it may be said, any wrong-doing is a menace to the general well-being, by example, suggestion, contagion, by lowering the moral standard, by setting or contributing to a bad fashion. The reply is that the proper defence against this mode of attack is that which relies on the force of reason and will. The sin does not spread beyond the sinner unless we choose to let it do so, and as for the sinner himself, force will not convert him. With the invasion of a right it is otherwise. I cannot retain physical possession of my watch and purse if the thief has obtained physical possession of them. One or other of us must have them and not both, and if it is for the general well-being that that which I have come to posses on certain conditions should be secured to me, then the violation of this security should be prevented. The community might leave me—as many simple societies do—to vindicate my right by myself. It would still be necessary to vindicate it by prevention or by exacting reparation, that is by putting force upon the aggressor. It makes no difference whether it is private of public rights that are attacked A nation at war, if sufficiently confident of itself and its cause, and sufficiently imbued with the spirit of freedom, will tolerate reasoned arguments for peace, but it will not allow a man to show a light during an air raid on the ground that he conscientiously objects to participating in any organized method of defence. In the former case the majority have the cure in their own hands. They can retain their own opinion and act upon it none the less vigorously because a few disagree.[1] In the latter case their lot is bound up with that of the aggressor, and the light which he shows may bring the bombs on their roofs. Thus the moral wrong of bad action is to be met by moral means and the physical wrong by physical means. Opinions and with them actions that invade no right of others are free. Actions that do invade rights are not free. This distinction, drawn from the point of view of the individual agent, coincides closely with the distinction drawn from the point of view of associated action between cases when universal conformity is necessary for a specific purpose and cases where the common purpose may be achieved without calling on any but a willing co-operation. Broadly, these distinctions mark out the appropriate sphere of liberty from that of coercion.

Since a right is itself normally a liberty, it follows that the doctrine that liberty is limited by rights is not very remote from the suggestion that it is limited by the like liberty of others. The essential differences are three. Instead of the "like" liberty which we easily saw to be too simple, we must read "any one of a system of liberties." Secondly, this system cannot be defined by the individual himself for himself, but must be defined by or on behalf of the community on the basis of the general well-being. Thirdly, there are rights of the com-

---

[1] When Professor Ritchie (op. cit. p. 145) says "The right of making a speech . . . is limited by the goodwill of the society as a whole," may it not be replied that the goodness of the society's will in this relation may be measured by its readiness to suffer—and even attend to—speeches which it dislikes?

munity as an organized whole to be added to the rights which interest its members as individuals. Again, our principle puts the doctrine that self-regarding acts are free in the form that acts are free so far as they are self-regarding, and bases it not on the indifference of the community to the individual but on the need of the community for individual judgment and character, and the impossibility of building up character by coercion.

The doctrine that liberty is limited by private rights would hardly be contested in general terms by individualists. The cases in which difficulty arises are those in which men proceeding on one uncontested right invade another about which perhaps there is less unanimity. The classical case is that of free contract. Admittedly it is in general good that people should be able to enter into agreements for their mutual advantage, provided that no damage is inflicted on a third party. But this right may be used by a stronger party in a bargain to impose very disadvantageous terms on the weaker, with the result that the position of the weaker side undergoes progressive deterioration, and perhaps in the event a whole class enters into a kind of subjugation to another. The modern state has continually intervened to arrest this process, and this has been regarded possibly as good, possibly as evil, but in any case as a curtailment of liberty. This opinion rests on an excessive abstraction. In the first place there are other rights of individuals not less important than free contract—such as the right of a competent and willing worker to the minimum conditions of a civilized existence. In the second place— and this is more fundamental—freedom of contract is insufficiently defined when it is regarded as consisting solely in the absence of control. Freedom of contract implies such substantial equality between the parties as on the whole leaves to each a real choice between concluding and rejecting the bargain. Where no such equality exists one party acts under a degree of compulsion. Indeed pushed far enough the abstract principle of free contract may contradict itself, for it may allow (and at times has allowed) of a man's selling himself into slavery and thereby forfeiting all further freedom of contract in perpetuity. Free contract stands, like all other rights, in need of careful definition in all its bearings on the contracting parties and the good of the community.

The case of temptations to vice presents some analogies. The man who offers liquor to an habitual drunkard takes him at a disadvantage, and is morally more reprehensible than the drunkard himself. Sexual relations, whether regular or irregular, give rise in the same way to manifold forms of agreement, in which consent, now of one party, now of the other, may be given under a greater or less degree of constraint, and with a greater or less understanding of the consequences involved. In none of these cases is the consent of the weaker party a sufficient social justification of the relation. We move here in a borderland wherein we certainly cannot speak of a forcible or fraudulent invasion of rights, and yet a form of undue influence is used to the profit of one and the undoing of another. A man is attacked subtly and through his impulses and emotions and corrupted. Now we said above that moral damage ought to be met by moral means, that moral evil does not spread if our will and reason choose to combat it. But we must realize that there are limits to the power of will, and we must regard a man who deliberately plays upon the bad passions of another for his own ends as taking an undue advantage, and the sufferer as having a right to protest against such practices. From the nature of the case the limits of this right cannot be precisely defined by itself, but must be considered in relation to other rights. If for instance A, in the pursuit of an established right (as e.g. to state a case to the public) does or says something which is of injurious tendency to B's character, that is regrettable but not preventible. If, on the other hand, he goes about to play on B's passions for some ends of his own, it is treatment against which B should be protected.[1] If again

---

[1] Though ambiguous cases will still suggest themselves, the principle gives, I think, the true basis of the punishment of e.g. indecency. Blatant and public indecency is punishable merely as a nuisance. The question arises with regard e.g. to indecent publications which (it may be said) we are free to avoid if we choose. This is indeed to ignore the innocent purchaser, but putting that aside we have to ask on what grounds we do or should punish in such cases. Now, we do punish very often on the mere ground of dislike, and so perfectly genuine scientific analyses of sexual matters or quite serious pleas for unorthodox morals come under the police ban while deliberate indecency escapes. For if it comes to dislike the plain man hates and fears analysis or any reasoned doubt of his imbued opinion infinitely more than a naughty story or a risky play. Thus prosecution of expressions deemed immoral is intrinsically objectionable as the wrong principle. The just principle is prosecution of that which, while appealing to bad passions, is not sanctioned by any right to utter it, as, e.g., that it is in the interest of truth and of the public welfare as the writer conceives it.

82 THE ELEMENTS OF SOCIAL JUSTICE

A's right to shape his own life is to be limited by the possible effect of example on B, that is substantially to negate any right of A to depart from the social norm, and to withhold from B any stimulus to exert his own will-power in self-control. Both these results we have considered and dismissed as bad. On the other hand, to give B protection at a specific danger-point and to limit A's action accordingly is not, if the limit can be made sufficiently precise, either to withhold the general liberty or impair the general responsibility which are the things we value.[1]

Again, the right of association may be deduced from freedom of agreement. But the logical inference must not cause us to overlook the fact that a new social situation may be engendered by the relations, however voluntary, between two or more individuals. In relation to others an association may in fact exercise coercive powers which the individuals separately enjoying the same rights could not attain. Such powers must be

---

[1] All these cases fall within a region where the right of protection (as against temptation, bad example, etc.) is dubious because if generalized it militates against the development of personality by self-government. Hence if the counteracting claims (e.g. to defend an unpopular opinion or to order one's life without regard to the indirect effect of example) are as they are here conceived to be, essential elements of liberty, it is they that should be the governing consideration. We may afford a protection to the weaker vessel which does not sensibly impair them, but not more. This is merely to say that in case of conflict we should define the weaker and more doubtful right by reference to the more certain and important, and the statement above (pp. 40-41) that every right must in the end be defined in reference to any other that may impinge upon it should be taken with this rider.

regulated by the Common Good in each case. The association may be formed by the exercise of rights which it is good that its members should enjoy. But being formed, it has powers which those rights would not have given to its members taken severally. It is socially considered a new entity, and the question whether its powers are such as make for the Common Good is to be settled by considering not only how they were built up, but what they are and how they are exercised. We see from such cases that the extension of legal control is not necessarily a curtailment of liberty. It may be and often is a question of one constraint against another, the direct and open prohibition of some direct and less acknowledged use of power. It is not then a question of liberty in general against constraint in general but of one liberty against another or one constraint against another. Which of the two is to be preferred depends, as of course, on the conditions of the common welfare. Now the relevant conditions may be such as have no especial bearing upon liberty in general, e.g. they may be conditions of health, security, economic efficiency, etc. But it may be also that "Liberty" itself has something to say, i.e. of two alternative "liberties" one is of a higher kind or has a larger application. To illustrate these points we may take the early closing of shops. Efforts were made to establish a short day by agreement, but they failed because the refusal of a few, or even a single tradesman to conform, gave him an advantage in competition which enabled him to defeat the majority. In such a case it is useless to argue that the majority are at liberty to close early if they think fit.

In practice they are at the mercy of the minority. The majority can give effect to its will only by the aid of the law, or by organizing itself. On the surface the minority is coerced and liberty appears to suffer. But in the realities of the situation if the minority has its way, the majority is coerced. It is, therefore, a question not of liberty against constraint, but of one sort of constraint against another—the organized and direct against the indirect but not less real. So far the question which is right appears not as a question of liberty, but of which rule conforms to other conditions of the common welfare. If, however, we look a little further into this matter we see that the interests of liberty in general are affected in more than one way. To begin with we found that apart from regulation the few were able to obstruct and defeat the many, and that it was only by the aid of law (or possibly by their own organization) that the majority could get their way. Where that is the case it follows that regulation which looks at first sight like a mere restriction on liberty is in fact the method of securing the liberty of the greater number. But further in this case before us, we are not merely dealing with the liberty of the proprietors to open and close shops, but of employees to enjoy leisure. It is this liberty which has seemed the governing consideration to the community, and rightly, since a modicum of leisure is necessary to the development of mind and character. Now if this judgment is correct it is of far-reaching application. It explains how it is that there are "Liberties" which on the whole make for Liberty, and liberties which are on the whole unfavourable to

Liberty. That is to say, it suggests a principle which will answer our former question, "What is the bearing of Liberty on the body of restraints involved in the system of rights?" For by Liberty we see more and more clearly that we mean the open field for mind and character, and the rights that we maintain and the restrictions that we impose should so far as compatible with the other conditions of social organization be conceived in the interest of such development. Liberty so understood is itself the most far-reaching principle of the common welfare, in the name of which it is that restraints are imposed.[1]

In the matter of public right few would deny that the community has a right to protect itself. Few would deny that it must have some power to make and administer laws and regulations for the common weal. But there have been two sources of controversy. Some have seen in every new regulation a fresh restriction of lib-

[1] It is worth noting that in the case taken as an instance still further points of liberty may be involved. For example, the opening and closing of shops on a Saturday or Sunday involves points of religious observance and affects Jews, Christians and Freethinkers differently. When a regulation is made by or in the interests of a majority points of this kind may escape attention. It is not then fair to argue that the majority is merely vindicating to itself a liberty which would otherwise be denied to it. It is vindicating a liberty which involves perhaps the denial not only of the same, but also of quite another kind of liberty to its opponents, and this liberty may be far the more important of the two. Thus it is contrary to liberty to interfere with rights of religion or conscience on the ground of the mere administrative convenience of a simple common rule. Rules drawn with regard for liberty admit of variations and adapt them to the requirements of nonconforming bodies or individuals.

erty. This we have found to be incorrect. Some regulations are favourable to liberty and some unfavourable. We may revert to this point after considering the deeper issue, which arises when law and conscience come into conflict. If the common good rests on the spiritual nature of man, and if liberty is the condition under which this nature develops, what is to happen if that which the majority thinks right is that which the minority think wrong? If the majority can go on their way unimpeded, they have in our view no right of coercion. But if they cannot do so, if the conscientious non-conformity of a minority wrecks the plan which they no less conscientiously believe necessary to the common welfare, what is to be done? The question came to a head in the war in the requirement of military service. It was believed by some that any concession to the conscientious objector endangered the imposition of compulsory service, and thereby the safety of the nation. It is impossible to discuss the question of principle without remarking that in fact this opinion was never substantiated. Parliament, in passing the Military Service Acts, took a different view and made provision for exemption. But many tribunals, with no effective protest from public opinion, disregarded this provision in administration, and many conscientious objectors in consequence suffered prolonged and repeated terms of imprisonment. Under the circumstances, therefore, their treatment can only be termed an unjustifiable persecution. But this does not dispose of the problem in principle. Let us suppose a form of conscientious objection really fatal to collective efficiency. Let us assume that every way out of the *impasse* has been honourably tried and found unavailing. In such a case, can it be right to compel a man to do what he thinks wrong, or to seek to compel him by threats, and punish him if he persists in refusal? The relpy, however distasteful, must be that here again we are dealing with liberty against liberty, coercion against coercion. It is assumed that the governing power on its side is acting as conscientiously for what it holds right, i.e. necessary for the common well-being, as the individual on his side. It is assumed that the individual by his refusal can effectively thwart the governing power, compel it, that is to say, to abandon its end, or at lowest jeopardize the fruits of its effort. In this case once again, therefore, there is in the realities of the situation constraint on either side, and which side is right in using it can only be judged by him who can determine where the true conditions of the common welfare lie. The liberty which the individual retains to the last is that of protest. The liberty which the community vindicates in the end is that of action. The right of the individual and the duty of the community towards him is to treat him not as a common criminal but as a martyr. It is not debarred from imprisoning or even shooting him, but it is debarred from the use of the weapons of contumely, derision and defilement of character. With those limitations the hard saying must be accepted that it may be right to penalize a man for doing what he thinks right.[1]

---

[1] A fairly simple illustration may be accorded by religious bodies which disbelieve in the reality of disease and think it wrong to take measures of medical prevention or cure. A member of such a

We must not then allow the regard for liberty to deter us from repelling definite invasions of any of the conditions of the common welfare. But in any given case we must consider whether the methods of defence used violate in their turn some condition of the common welfare, and if so, whether the condition violated may not be more essential than that which is maintained. If so, we should put up with the minor evil, foregoing for example a point of general convenience in preference to violating a claim of conscience.

The hypothesis upon which the above argument proceeds, that the State acts bona fide and intelligently, is a large assumption, and one that is unfortunately too often out of accord with the facts. In its external relations the morality of a State is usually low, and it is largely of its own fault that it gets into difficulties from which it can only be rescued by calling on its members for great sacrifices. In internal relations it is improvident and clumsy. Hence we cannot in practice treat the actual rights of the State as equivalent to rights which the community might very properly exercise if it were adequately organized for the purpose of conducting its affairs in the best possible way. It has been absolutely necessary in modern times to extend the functions of the State in two directions. One is the better protection of personal rights—particularly in the economic sphere. The other is the organization of

community might go about with an infectious disease upon him, in which case the rest of the community who believe in the reality of infection would certainly be right from their point of view in shutting him up.

public resources for certain common objects, e.g. education and for the sharing of economic burdens and advantages as the Unemployment Insurance. Neither of these developments involves any true loss of personal liberty. The first is, as we have seen, a better definition of liberty. The second, if financed on a proper basis, is not (as will be seen later) a mulcting of individuals or a taxation of one class for the benefit of another, but an appropriation to common ends of wealth which arises out of common efforts. In these directions then personal life does not suffer from the extension of State functions. It is otherwise when the State enters upon the control of personal and family life, determines what men may buy and sell, restricts emigration and immigration, requires constant registration for all manner of reasons, develops a system of espionage and persecutes advanced opinion. Its motives may be good or bad, but the control of daily life, unless its object is to combat some private or sectional oppression, is clearly opposed to liberty, and in this relation the familiar antithesis of private liberty and governmental control is self-consistent and legitimate. The practical problem of modern domestic politics is to secure the benefits of organization and the maintenance of all personal rights against private oppression, without sacrificing not less valuable private rights to the ubiquitous encroachments of State authority. The practical solution must lie mainly in the development of better organs of government, but one step towards clearing the issue is the definition of liberty. We have been too much under the influence of a simple opposition between personal liberty and State control.

There are (as urged here) other enemies of liberty besides the State, and it is in fact by the State that we have fought them. Hence conversely much of the extension of State authority has been friendly to liberty, but it by no means follows that other extensions will be of the same kind. Liberty is neither for nor against the power of the State as such, but for the direction of its power towards the maintenance and development of personal rights and away from the attempt to control opinion, govern personal life and direct the general course of production[1] and exchange.

We see before us then the answer to our two questions as to the ultimate basis of liberty and as to the part which it plays in determining the rights by which it is conditioned. The ultimate foundation of liberty is that it is a condition of spiritual growth. This is the "general" liberty underlying, inspiring, and also transcending all "liberties." But there would be no liberty for us all if any fool, rogue, or fire-eater had liberty for his part to develop his folly, roguery, or violence at our expense. Very possibly his own spiritual development might be best served by playing the game to the end and realizing at long last its fatuity. But in the meanwhile what of the lives of others, that he has wrecked? It is here that physical restraint becomes necessary and that "liberty" must be particularized into "liberties." Lib-

[1] This may be maintained without prejudice to the question discussed later, whether the State should control or itself organize the production of certain necessaries or other articles in general demand. The point of freedom is (1) that men should be able to buy what they will, where they will, and (2) that there should be plenty of scope for initiative in production.

LIBERTY

erty—we come back to the initial paradox—itself demands restraints. In the name of liberty we must restrain people from interfering with expressions of character and opinion as expressions of character and opinion. In general we must restrain them from violating anything that we take to be an essential condition of the common wellbeing that is a right, while unless and until we define such a right we ought not to restrain them by other than moral methods. Further, rights, properly regarded, are not mere restrictions of liberty from without but so many definitions of the liberty which having in view the ends of associated life, can be enjoyed by all members of a community alike. True, any general condition of health, wealth and welfare may be the foundation of a duty and a right, and it is with reference to these ends and not to liberty alone that many rights are defined. But the bare idea of right is essential to liberty, for it is the distinctive value of a right (as opposed to a prescribed duty) that it is a basis upon which its possessor constructs his own course of action having therein a measure of initiative and free choice.[1] Thus we have rights as well as duties, because we need liberty, and the system of rights is the system of harmonized liberties. Finally in shaping this system the requirements of spiritual

---

[1] It may be asked whether this conception of a sphere of freedom for the individual is compatible with obligation on all men to do their utmost for the Common Good. The reply in general terms is, that all men ought to do their utmost for what is good, but within limits it is right that each should judge for himself what that utmost is, and by what method it is to be achieved. It is here, too, that the true ethical difference between rights and duties and between duties of perfect and imperfect obligation survives. Society

growth form the highest consideration, and spiritual liberty not least among them. Putting one restraint against another, that restraint which sets the life of mind free is preferred by Liberty. Liberty then is the inspiration of the body of rights, though in their detailed determination all conditions of the common welfare are involved.

In more general terms, Liberty is both the effect and the cause of social harmony. It is the effect because, as shown at the outset, anarchy and repressive order alike involve frustration of will, while it is only in proportion as they come into spontaneous accord with one another that wills can be fully free. It is the cause because harmony is in the largest sense a spiritual achievement, the achievement of mental energy self-disciplined in co-operative unity, and this self-discipline is Liberty.

In this conception of Liberty it is not suggested that the development of any individual is a matter of indifference to the community. His conduct is left to his judgment in so far as it does not interfere with the rights of others, on the ground (*a*) that his personal development is only to be sought through his own rational choice, and (*b*) that it is generally by the cultivation

as a whole has always a right to our best efforts, and to put them forward is always a matter of perfect obligation. But in some respects it defines the direction of these efforts—by specifying rights of others, or rights of its own body. These constitute duties of so-called perfect obligation, or as they should rather be termed, "specific duties." In other respects it leaves it to us to define them, and our duty to it is then to use our judgment to the best of our powers. Liberty of conscience has as its obverse the obligation of conscientiousness.

of personality in this sense that the Common Good is developed. The obverse of this principle is the right and duty of tutelage over the individual whose judgment is immature or impaired. Thus it is the right of the child to receive, and therefore a duty of the community to secure to it, the education necessary to bring the mind to the maturity at which it is capable of forming a judgment. Beyond this there is a right and duty of tutelage over the permanently incapable. But this obligation needs careful definition. We must not construe it as a general duty of the stronger mind to judge for the weaker, which would be contrary to all the conditions of personal development that have been laid down. The sounder method is to rely on the educational power of freedom and responsibility and extend them always to the farthest possible limit. A man should only be in permanent tutelage who is permanently incapable of self-control.

On the same principle, however, temporary control would seem to be justified where the passions of a moment interfere with the development of a life and where impulses overwhelm the judgment. So far as momentary impulses are concerned this is generally true, but we cannot overlook the difficulty that the strongest of all passions may permanently modify character and so govern deliberate choice. In this connection we may be tempted to regard ill-conduct as *eo ipso* proof of mental or moral incapacity. But so to argue is to lay ourselves open to the charge—which we have hitherto rebutted—of assuming infallibility. For we use divergence of judgment as itself a proof of weakness of judgment.

We are not content to say that he who differs from us errs—which is indeed implied in the fact that we retain our own opinion—but we assign as ground of the difference an intrinsic feebleness of judgment, and such an imputation based on such a ground is a tacit assumption of intrinsic certainty in our judgment differing only in degree from infallibility. The proofs of mental defect must be in something other than difference of opinion. They must lie in the criteria accepted by the alienist of incapacity to appreciate or be guided by the consequences of actions. It is not questioned that conduct injurious to self may simply, as injurious to self and apart from all other considerations, be immoral. But it is urged that unless there is evidence of such an incapacity for a rational self-control as to justify a state of tutelage, the appropriate method of dealing with such wrong-doing is that of rational influence, not of coercive control. This view rests on the true nature of personal morality, which consists not in the preventing of overt acts by nonmoral motives—and the motive is equally non-moral whether it be the fear of a social boycott or of prison—but in the dominance of the social personality through the education of the feelings and the reason. It is supported also by the consideration that morality which at its best consists essentially, not in mutual censorship but in the sense of fellowship to which censoriousness is hostile. Tutelage, then, is applicable as a permanent condition only to those who are mentally incapable of entering into such a fellowship, and as a temporary expedient to those occasions on which an impulsive act of folly might ruin a life.

The main results of our argument may now be summarily stated.

Man needs liberty as the basis of rational self-determination because this lies at the root of all spiritual development. In society this takes the two forms of growth of character through self-control and of social wisdom through mental intercourse. Liberty as a social ideal is scope for such a development.

In organized society such liberty is made possible by the establishment of a body of rights which are at once "liberties" and restraints. Each right is defined by some element of common welfare which it serves, and of this the requirements of spiritual development form an essential part.

By rights so determined, and by them only, freedom of action is to be defined and limited. There is no restraint where there is no invasion, coercive or fraudulent, of some right. Protection in doubtful cases, i.e. tutelage, is subject to the condition that the fundamental rights of self-expression and interchange of ideas are not sensibly impaired.

Our discussion has dealt with the relations of the individual and the community. It has taken law and government as standing for the community, and has in general assumed their *bona fides* in so doing. We have not inquired into the guarantees of this relation; we have not, that is to say, asked how far or under what conditions it is in fact the case, that law and government do represent either the will or the good of the community. Yet this question involves the problem of political freedom in one of the most commonly accepted usages of that term. A community is regarded as politically free on condition, not only that it is independent of others, but that its own constitution rests on a wide if not a universal suffrage. There are questions concerned with political rights which it will be well to take by themselves, but the general principle of political democracy—and something more—has in fact been implied in our account of liberty. For we have conceived the genuine basis of liberty as a harmony to which the life of every person concerned is a contributory factor. It follows that free institutions are those which arise out of the character and will of all the individuals who live under them by a process of growth. In this growth the exercise of political rights is but an occasional, though a necessary, incident, while freedom of opinion, and, within the limits defined, of action, are factors continuously at work. Political freedom in the narrower sense is the right of contributing by voice and vote to the explicit decisions, laws and administrative acts, which bind the community. To say that in virtue of this contribution the collective decisions express the will of each citizen even if he has done his best to prevent it, is a highly misleading piece of rhetoric which may be turned to harsh and cruel purposes.[1] Political freedom, precisely because it is the common freedom of many, gives no such absolute liberty and therefore no such responsibility to any one man. Political freedom is just the right of every man bound by decisions to contribute whatever it is in him to con-

[1] As for example, if every German (including children born after 1914) is held responsible for the war, or every Englishman for the outrages committed by the irregular police in Ireland.

tribute to the making and remaking of those decisions. It by no means guarantees that he will be bound only by his own will. It guarantees that his will is to count among the rest in making the decisions, and that the community as a whole will be bound by the main current of will flowing within it, the resultant of all the wills and brains of every one concerned in proportion to the energy and intelligence which he brings to bear. That the collective actions should in this manner express the prevalent wills of the community and not be imposed on them is essential to the completion of the principle of Harmony.

Political liberty, so often spoken of as a guarantee to the individual of his other rights, in reality secures very little to the individual as such, precisely because it has to be shared with so many. It is a guarantee to the whole community that it will not be governed by any outside power or by any individual or section of its own members. It is a guarantee to a sufficiently large group or interest that its claims will be heard and its wishes made themselves felt. But to the individual as such it is rather a duty than a privilege, rather a function than a new possession. At bottom perhaps it is most important as a recognition of his full memebrship of the community, and the enfranchisement of a class or sex has its most decisive effect not so much in the particular men or measures for whom the new votes are cast as in a subtler and more pervasive change in the whole attitude of government to that class, and of the class to the community. It is for the first time absorbed in spirit as an active working partner with the common life. Of course this implies more than the mere possession of a vote. It implies that the vote is used, and becomes the pivot of an extended political education. But the beginning of this education is the bare recognition that the newly enfranchised are not merely passive subjects, but active citizens, with functions to perform as well as benefits to secure from their participation in the common life.

It is in its political aspect that liberty reveals itself most clearly in its essence as the education of the social will. A community is free in the degree in which will replaces force as the basis of social relations, and this again means the degree in which a fundamental harmony is established as a firm basis of co-operation underlying all divergence of individual and sectional desire. The prime condition of such harmony is what we may call the Right of Reason, which is that desires should be free to express themselves, that opinions should be heard, claims considered, and decisions taken on discussion. The second condition is that when a claim is rejected and the freedom of an individual curtailed, this should be done in the name of the Common Good and not of any private or personal preference. Thirdly, the Common Good rests on the enlargement of mind and development of character throughout the community, which in turn depends on freedom in thought and responsibility in action. Hence the restraints required by the common good take the form of a system of rights which defines the field of liberty, and where no right is invaded there is no restriction. Lastly, since our understanding of the Common Good and its true conditions is imperfect, there must be the continuous right of criticism and amendment, which brings us back to our first principle of the rights of Reason. We defined Liberty at the outset negatively as the absence of external constraint, positively as self-determination. Our discussion of social liberty has shown that the two definitions are intelligible and applicable if taken in close connection with one another. There must be restraints in any society, but in a free community they are those which human wills in co-operation impose on themselves for the sake of their common end, and, since this end is a Harmony, in proportion as it is approached the restraints are merged in willing acceptance. Thus the principle of Liberty is a project of social harmony and the realization of liberty the measure of its success. In more exact analysis the end is the harmonious energizing of Mind in the plenitude of its development, and this implies the overcoming of all external constraint and the transformation even of self-restraint into the hearty acceptance of the larger life, that is to say into unimpeded self-determination.

How Liberty withers under civilization, how the individual is lost in the crowd and smothered under the vast apparatus of modernity, how he sighs for the simple life and untrammelled self-dependence of the savage is an old story. It is also an old illusion. One of the few generalizations that emerge clearly from the study of archaic cultures and of the simpler peoples is that in "primitive" society men are unfree. They may not be servants of a master, but they are in bondage to custom and, as a rule, to complex and minute codes of custom imposing restrictions which the supposed slave of civilization would find equally irksome and irrational. The simplest communities do indeed enjoy so much of freedom as is involved in living in accordance with their own customs and traditions untrammelled by a superior, but they do not know that freedom of the spirit which would prompt them to the reorganization of their customs for the betterment of their lives. Within them the individual has but little scope. The lines of his life are determined by his position in this or that kindred, totem-group or marriage-class, and what liberty he enjoys is that of being let alone by a society which knows little of any organized effort. With the development of military and economic organization even these elements are weakened or lost. Distinctions of class and caste arise. Slavery helotage or serfdom make their appearance. There is more of organization and order, but they are based on the principle of subordination. The history of liberty as a principle of high social organization begins only with the emergence of the civic state,[1] and we may here cast a cursory glance at the main stages of its march. To the Greek of the classical period Liberty meant first and foremost the autonomy of the city state as against subjection to Persia, to Athens or to Sparta. Secondly, within the State it meant the rule of law: "Though the Lacedemonians are free, yet they are not free in all things, for over them is set law as a master whom they

[1] In the vaunted freedom of the Teutonic tribes the student of the simpler societies will see rather the embers of primitive resistance to organized unity than the first gleam of ordered liberty.

fear much more even than thy people fear thee."[1] "He who bids intelligence rule seems to bid God and the laws rule, but he who bids man adds beast as well. For that is the nature of appetite, and passion distorts rulers, even the best men. Wherefore the law is intelligence without desire."[2] As a consequence freedom meant the status of a citizen clothed with full legal rights and duties—the antithesis of a slave, and this and no more is meant when e.g. freedom is said to be the basis of civic privileges. Thirdly, for the individual political freedom meant a positive share in self-government, the power to rule and be ruled with a view to life at its best. Fourthly, in Aristotle at least we have the conception of differentiation as in itself a good thing— "to unify too much is not so well."

These are the elements of civic and political liberty. With the Cynics and Stoics begins an assertion of spiritual and "natural" freedom. The wise man rules himself by his conscious and deliberate acceptance of the law of nature, which is the law of God. He must be first and above all things the captain of his own soul, and for the sake of this captaincy must stand against father, wife, magistrate or emperor, seeking refuge if need be in death. But a keener edge was to be given to this sword of the spirit by the development of Christianity. Monotheism, from its nature, could know none of the easy tolerance of earlier religions. Its claims were as absolute as they were mutually opposed, and each man's duty to his faith, his Church, and finally

[1] Demaratus to Xerxes, *Herodotus* 7, 104 (tr. Macaulay).
[2] Aristotle, *Politics,* III. xvi. 3.

to his own conscience, became his supreme law; out of the largest claims of spiritual authority emerged the deepest sense of a sovereign responsibility that was inward and personal. The early Protestant reformers, indeed, were far from being aware of the path on which they were entering, and I cannot here attempt to sketch the process by which from toleration as a practical necessity of politics men advanced to the conception of liberty as the basis of spiritual experience and the guardian of spiritual truth. This conception, as shown above, is the life-breath of modern liberty and the sustaining force of the political struggle.

In this struggle the first step was to reassert the supremacy of law. "Freedom of men under government," writes Locke, "is to have a standing rule to live by, common to every one of that society and made by the legislative power erected in it."[1] This was the Greek principle, only here law is not itself liberty, but an instrument of liberty, a means of its equable adjustment among all members of the community, and above all to its secure enjoyment. This relation was first seen as an antithesis between positive law and natural right which led, as we have seen, to undue restriction of law and liberty alike. It needed experience to show that in the service of a fuller liberty law must in some directions be extended, that collective restraint and common liberty are two sides of the same thing, and that the system of assured rights is the body of which liberty is the soul.

We cannot here attempt any measure of the advance

[1] *Second Treatise on Civil Government,* chap. iv.

which Liberty had made by 1914. In the personal, economic and constitutional sphere it was undoubtedly great. The difficulties which had arisen were those of nationality on the one hand and inter-state anarchy—with militarism as its reverse aspect—on the other. Nor is it yet possible to decide whether the subsequent decline of Liberty is temporary or permanent. This must be for the historian of fifty years hence to say—if he is still allowed to say it. For the present we observe only that as the security of Law was the first thing to be won so it is among the first to be lost, but its loss carries every right away with it in a common ruin.

CHAPTER V

JUSTICE AND EQUALITY

Justice is a name to which every knee will bow. Equality is a word which many fear and detest. Yet the just was rightly declared by Aristotle to be a form of the equal. How is this difference of authority to be explained? What is justice in a community, and assuming that by the term we mean the right ordering of human relations, what is its true connection with equality?

Before we can answer that question we must know what equality means. What is intended when the term is used of human beings?

In point of fact there are some conceptions of human equality which are at least *prima facie* tenable, and others which have only to be stated clearly to be dismissed from serious discussion. Thus the famous principle "All men are by nature equal," has two possible meanings. It may mean that men are by nature endowed with equal gifts or innate capacities. This is an allegation of fact which is untrue. It may, on the other hand, mean that all have equal rights, and this is an allegation of ethical principle that at least merits examination. This is, in fact, the assertion of the French Constituent Assembly, whose famous declaration runs, "All men are by nature free and equal in respect of their rights. Distinctions can only be founded on public utility."

We may cavil at the words "are by nature" as containing some unproven and unprovable allegation of fact, but whatever nature may be, or may have been supposed to be, it is clear that what is founded on it is not equality of endowment, but equality of right, and it is this claim which we have to consider. It is in respect of their rights that men are said to be equal, and it is this saying which must be tested.

But the question may be raised, Could men be equal even in respect of their rights if there were not some fundamental equality in their natural or inherent constitution? Have animals rights, and if so, are they of the same kind as those of men? Have inanimate things rights? In fact, is not a "right" a property of a rational, social, moral being, and if we admit this, can we maintain equality of rights without coming back to an allegation of fact in the shape of equality in natural, social or moral capability?

The reply to this is first, that on the principle of harmony every being that can feel has rights in the sense that it is entitled to consideration. Its happiness or comfort is, so far as it goes, a part of the good, and its pain and misery of the bad. Secondly, as a matter of the interpretation of experience, there is something peculiar to human beings and common to human beings without distinction of class, race or sex, which lies far deeper than all differences between them. Call it what we may, soul, reason, the abysmal capacity for suffering, or just human nature, it is something generic, of which there may be many specific, as well as quantitative differences, but which underlies and embraces them all. If this common nature is what the doctrine of equal rights postulates, it has no reason to fear the test of our ordinary experience of life, or of our study of history and anthropology.

That men have certain fundamental rights as men, and apart from every other consideration, is then, at any rate, an intelligible proposition. On the other hand, the simple generalization that all men have equal rights, taken as it stands, would make a hash of all social relations. A convicted murderer would then stand on the same footing as the most harmless citizen, and a child would have no more claim on his mother than on any chance comer. Some doctrines of philosophical anarchy may have played with this conception, but it is not that which is intended by most advocates of equal rights. They would, I think, generally recognize that men stand in very various relations. Some of these they find "given," e.g. the parental tie. Others they make for themselves, e.g. the marriage tie, or any contractual obligation. These various relations carry their specific rights and duties; rights and duties, therefore, which are not the same for all men, but distinguish those within the relation from those without. In this regard, the principle of equal rights has two applications. First, it insists that the special obligation applies impartially to all who fall under it. If the contract is binding on the one side it is binding on the other—a platitude perhaps when put in abstract terms, but in actual life a principle by no means without point. Secondly, it insists that so far as these special relations are created by the acts of men, all men have a right to enter into them, e.g. that all men have a right to enter into contracts, to acquire and hold property, to marry, to have children, and so forth. Equality in this respect—equal opportunity or equal freedom—has, in fact, been the main bone of contention in the past. The right to make contracts or to hold property has often enough been denied, or only granted with severe reservations, to women, or to slaves or serfs. Freedom of choice in marriage has been denied. The right of migration has been denied. The choice of occupation has been denied. Finally, the modern state, after abolishing most of the older restrictions in these respects, has begun to impose new restrictions of its own. It is clear, therefore, that at this point we touch one of the live questions of equality, and one closely interwoven with questions of liberty. For the moment, we are not concerned with the answer to the question, but only with the question itself. That is to say, we are concerned to find a meaning for "human equality" which will at least bear investigation. For this purpose, we discard "equality of endowment" and bare equality of right, and adopt equality in some fundamental rights, including (among others as yet unspecified) the right of enjoying and entering into special relations, carrying special rights impartially maintained.

So far we have started from common human nature, and treated differences as secondary. There is another way of regarding equality which begins with the differences, and regards equality as essentially an adjustment in which differences of persons (in whatever respect) is made a basis of corresponding differences of treatment. The "equality" of this doctrine is not an equality of absolute magnitude, but of proportion. "Injustice," says

Aristotle, who is the father of this conception, "arises when equals are treated unequally, and also when unequals are treated equally." Justice is an equality of proportion between persons and "things" assigned to them. The "things" here may be office, honour, rank, money, or any of the objects of human desire. These should be distributed, not equally, but in proportion to some quality, character or achievement of the persons concerned. What is this quality? Aristotle points out that the basis of distribution adopted differs in different states, or as we might say, in different social systems. It may be birth, rank or office (τίμη), or (as in what Aristotle calls an oligarchy) wealth. It may be simply the status of a free man (as in a Greek democracy), and then the rule of proportion fails, and absolute or "arithmetic" equality is substituted. Lastly, it may, and according to Aristotle ought to be, merit (ἀξία). The equality of distributive justice, then, is for Aristotle an equality in the proportion of merit to rights.

With Aristotle's principle we may approximately contrast the preference of the English nobleman for the Order of the Garter as a distinction, "because there was no damned nonsense about merit in it.", Aristotle is clearly right in pointing out that actual social systems have their own characteristic grounds of proportionment. When we find that the British Naval Prize regulations assigned one share to the common seaman, and so many more to each higher rank culminating in four thousand shares for the admiral, we may, with all respect for admiralship, infer that this proportion reflects not so much a computation of the respective value of services rendered as the consideration that admiral and seaman are men of different birth and status accustomed to completely different standards of wealth. The function of the admiral is no doubt vastly the more important, but the difference is hardly one that admits of arithmetical computation, and the ratio of four thousand to one means, I fear, that the admiral belonged to the class which enforced the rate and the seaman to the class which had to take what it could get.

There are other possible bases of differentiation besides desert. But, with one exception, I do not propose to examine them, as they seem to be rather principles of inequality than of equality. And the view of justice which will emerge as we proceed will be found to justify the economy of space in ignoring them. One remark only may be made. Under a social system a man or men in such and such a position finds such and such things due to him. Given the social system, it is just that he should enjoy these things. The law allows it and the court awards it. It is not just to deprive him of them, leaving the rest of the social system standing. But if the justice of the social system itself be in question these considerations have no relevance; and in a general inquiry into justice social systems are, in fact, as much in question as anything else.

Returning then to proportionate equality, let us consider desert as a basis of differentiation. It may be remarked first that proportion seems to imply quantitative measurement. Now there are cases in which quantitative measurement is readily applicable. If A works for one hour and B for two on the same task and with the same effort and skill, it is on the face of it reasonable that B should be paid twice as much as A. Even here various difficulties arise when we look closer. For example, under a modern wages agreement, if A works eight hours and B works nine, it is probable that for the ninth hour B will get "time-and-a-quarter." But to pass over these minor points for a moment, consider the incommensurable factors. A has routine work, B a skilled job, C hard taxing toil, D intermittent occasion for highly responsible decisions. There is no clear quantitative proportion between the various qualities engaged such as would be reflected, for example, in proportionate rates of payment. Aristotle, if the point had been put to him, would probably have replied that the distinction was certainly qualitative, and that each quality must receive as its due the conditions suited to its exercise. A modern economist would find a common money measure in the higgling of the market. He would say that the comparative scarcity of the quality required relatively to the demand for it would determine its marginal price, that is to say, the price that must be paid for the most elementary form of that quality which it is worth while to bring into operation, and that higher grades of the quality will obtain rewards proportional to their superiority. Thus, there are comparatively few men who can be trusted with responsibility, or who care to take it on any large scale, and so those who can be trusted get a high price, and the more successful they are the higher the price. Of the two replies, the one imputed to Aristotle (as being in the spirit though not the letter of his discussion) is more suggestive of principle, but gives no actual determination of a quantitative kind. The economists' version gives a quantitative determination, but bases it on the hard facts of the human market rather than on ethical principle.

We must return upon this difficulty at a later stage. But waiving it for the moment, and treating all desert as somehow commensurable, we have next to ask what desert itself means. Is it effort or result? Here is Jones, a faithful, industrious soul, who toils conscientiously and produces little. There is Smith, an unconscionable "slacker," who has the knack of turning off without apparent effort just what is needed. What are the relative deserts of Jones and Smith? Morally, I suppose, our sympathies go out to Jones. But let us suppose a third party, Brown, as industrious as Jones and as clever as Smith. His output will greatly exceed that of either of them, and it would hardly seem right that the difference should go unrecognized. Lastly, let us suppose they are all making a certain article for sale. Does it matter to a fourth party, Robinson, whether this article were made painfully by Jones in two hours, or easily by Smith (who idled the other hour) in one, or is it one of two articles made in the two hours by Brown? It is just the article that Robinson wants. How it is made is not (as purchaser) his concern, and there can only be one price for the product. Thus from one point of view, desert seems to be measured by effort, from another point of view by results. From one point of view, it seems just to reward and encourage effort, from another to secure to each man the whole product of his labour. On principles of proportionate equality either plan may be forcibly argued, and I do not think we can decide between them till we have considered the whole meaning of justice.

Whichever view we take, it must be clear that the principle of desert does not cover all rights. Babies in arms have rights, though they have not had time to show their deserts. Criminals forfeit certain rights as their punishment specifies. But no one, since the penalty of outlawry disappeared, is held to become altogether rightless, even if he is condemned to death. Unless these principles of the modern state are altogether unsound, it results that if some rights are contingent on services or liable to forfeiture by crime or neglect, there are others which attach to a member of the community, or even to a human being as such.

In respect of these rights, however, there is not necessarily an absolute equality. One well-known principle of equality is "to each according to his needs," which strictly taken is a proportionate not an absolute principle. A rationing system takes account of the different quantities of food required by a hard worker, a light worker, a man, a woman, or a child. The State owes protection to all its members alike, but may have to spend much more to secure it in a disturbed district than in a London suburb. Further, as the cost of satisfying any given need varies from case to case, so also does the urgency of different needs. Men have a real need of beauty, but it is not so urgent and pressing as their need of food, and it is reasonable to hold that the claim of a need is proportioned to its urgency. We may then regard even the most universal of common rights of man as propor-

JUSTICE AND EQUALITY 113

tioned to their needs, and if we understand proportion in the Aristotelian sense, which includes the qualitative as well as quantitative adaptation of treatment to the various requirements of cases, we may conveniently bring the different conceptions of equality which survive preliminary examination into one formula. We then obtain these propositions:—

1. By equality is meant equality of proportion between claims and satisfaction.
2. Claims are based either on need or desert. On the one view equal needs, on the other equal desert requires equal satisfaction.
3. Desert may be measured by effort or attainment. These principles are of general application. But further, men are born or enter into special relations to particular people. In regard to these equality means:
4. (*a*) Equal reciprocal obligation on all parties to the relation of equal cogency.
   (*b*) Equal opportunity to all to enter into such special relations as are constituted by human choice.

Such, I think, are conceptions of equality, which are *prima facie* tenable, as an element in a desirable social system. Divergent as they are in some material respects, I think they start from a common principle. A man's rights depend on his personality. They may be held to attach to personality as such, that is in effect to its needs. They may be held qualified by what the man has done, is doing, or about to do, that is by desert. Desert may be measured by effort of will or by the achievement which rests on other qualities which will cannot command, but in any case it is a function of personality. Lastly, a man's personal relations to another person may affect his obligations. But in relation to persons, all that is outside personality is extraneous and irrelevant, and to admit it is to admit inequality. This is, I think, the fundamental equalitarian conception in relation to persons.[1]

It need hardly be remarked that the alternatives are not necessarily exclusive. For example, need and desert might both enter into consideration, and in desert both effort and attainment. But in simply considering what is meant by equality we must distinguish. Thus the rewards allotted for two services may be in equal proportion (1) to the effort made, (2) to the value of the work done, or (3) to the needs of the performers. In

---

[1] Similarly, if it be justice as between communities that is in question, it may be held that a community has rights as such, or that its rights are qualified by its character as a community or by its special relations to other communities. But anything that ignores or overrides the claim of community, i.e. anything other than a rule applicable to any community similarly constituted and circumstanced, is irrelevant and the source of inequality. Lastly, a corresponding conception applies to elements or functions in the social life. A function has its due sphere defined by its relation to the common life as a whole, i.e. by any consideration arising from the nature of the function itself, or by any principle applied impartially to all functions, but not by any extraneous consideration, and not on any partial ground inconsistently applied. Thus underlying great divergence of possible application, there appears in the general conception of equality something applicable to all aspects of social life.

JUSTICE AND EQUALITY

each case there is a certain equality, but in each case it is computed on a different basis. What we have now to consider is the bearing of these principles on the rule of justice.

It may help us here to take a preliminary view of the kind of equality maintained in law. This is a point to which those who deny all value to equality seem hardly to have attended. Whatever else it may be, law is a rule couched in universal terms and applied impartially, that is, with accurate equality, to all cases that fall within its definitions. The law may be good or bad. The definition may be wide and abstract, or concrete and elaborate in its differentiations. As judged by an ethical standard, the rule itself may be just or unjust. It may apply to all men as men, or it may differentiate between one class and another. But within the terms of its definition it is a universal rule impartially applicable. The law may prescribe that all murderers should be hanged, or that only murder with premeditation is a capital offence, or (like some archaic laws) that murder of a noble by a commoner is capital while murder of a commoner by a noble is commutable. But in every case the rule is universal for the cases to which it applies, and this means that all persons whose cases conform to the rule are treated equally.

The equality before the law which most modern States boast goes farther than this. It not only applies its rules impartially, but in framing its rules it generally treats certain fundamental rights and duties as pertaining to all human beings, irrespective of rank, age, sex, race and even citizenship. In this respect it differs materially from the laws of many archaic States, and even of some more recent civilizations. Under such laws cases of homicide, for example, are distinguished according as slayer or slain is high caste or low caste, noble, free or slave, man or woman, of the same or of different kindred, citizen or alien. Equality before the law as a modern understands it, means not merely that the penalties attached to a case of homicide, whatever they may be, will be impartially enforced, but that the penalties will be the same whoever and whatever the slayer and the slain may be. It means equal protection of life and limb for every one under the law, and equal penalties on every one violating them. Protection of person and property may be said to be generally regarded as the equal right of all in modern law, though there may as a fact be some relations in which it is still inadequately enforced. On the other hand, the law also recognizes special relations with special obligations. It could not in fact recognize the general rights of property without maintaining the special rights of the owner of a particular property, or the general sanctity of contracts without enforcing the particular rights and duties of the parties to a particular contract. It may also confer special rights or impose special duties on certain classes, e.g. employers, or landlords, or trade unions. But in general all special rights and duties are subordinate to the common obligations. Thus a contract is void if it binds a man to an illegal act, and if any special legislation is deemed contrary to the general rights of the subject it is severely called in question. Thus it is in the spirit of modern law to hold certain fundamentals of right and duty equally applicable to all human beings, while special obligations are developed by their application to the varying relations of men and particular requirements of the common good. In this manner does law interpret equality.

Ethically the impartiality of law may be criticized on grounds of equity. It may be urged that individual cases falling within the same general definition will differ widely, and whatever law may do, ethics should have regard to the peculiarities of the case. Thus (the argument may proceed) equality is only a rough rule of social convenience, while the higher justice differentiates. To this contention the sufficient reply was given by Aristotle that while equity is undoubtedly the rectification of those shortcomings of law which proceed from its abstract character, it is the rectification for which the law-giver himself, had he "been there present," and considered the circumstances of the case, would have provided. The treatment which is truly equitable admits of formulation in a universal rule, though one which is more particular in its specifications than the abstract and general rule which it corrects. If it is equitable to excuse this criminal because he acted in a fit of passion, then it is unjust to subject such another to the full penalty who also acted in a fit of passion. We must either be prepared to go through with our exception and erect it into a universal and binding rule, or admit that our decision, while perhaps commending itself to some emotion, is none the less unjust, and it is unjust precisely in so far as it involves an ungrounded inequality.

Under the authority of law, then, rules are applied impartially under conditions which they themselves define, and on those conditions mete out to individuals gain or loss, good or evil, as the case may be. Now the rules themselves may be wise or unwise, just or unjust. If they are such as to serve the common good, and are, in fact, the most effective that can be devised for the purpose, they are wise and good, and if the just is a good and anything other than the rules would be less good, we must call them just. Justice in this sense is the impartial application of a rule founded on the common good. The reason for terming it just instead of merely good is its impartiality, i.e. a form of equality. But this equality, under the very divergent conditions that arrive out of the complexities of life, may involve all sorts of inequalities of treatment. For instance, when law or custom recognizes the ties of kinship, it does not insist, e.g., that an intestate estate should revert to the community at death, so that all should have an equal share in its enjoyment, but that it should go to the heirs recognized in the proportions laid down by rules which it will apply impartially to all estates. Custom and sentiment do not require that I should mete out to any chance comer that which I would give to my son, but rather that all men should observe a certain special standard in relation to their sons. The justification of all such specific rules of law, custom or sentiment, is that taken as a whole they work harmoniously, the variety of human activities, and the prescribed relation of feelings and dealings being such as on the whole to make the best life for the community. Thus, notwithstanding all impartiality in the application of rules, there may be great variety in the dealings which they contemplate, and this variation will be just by our definition if in sum it works for the common good.

So far justice appears as something purely dependent on, or derivative from, the Common Good. But we must now ask whether there is not a sense in which justice enters into the Common Good, and so has a hand in prescribing some if not all of the rules laid down. If that is so, justice will have a double function in social ethics. Generically it is that kind of equality which is essential to the common good, but this equality will figure on the one hand as impartiality in the application of rules, on the other as some constituent of the common good on which the rules are ethically based. To determine whether it does so figure we must examine more closely the principles which justice embodies and their relation to the principle of harmony.

The fundamental principle of justice is simply that moral judgments are universal. That which itself, without further qualifications or conditions, is good, is good universally, that which in the same way is bad is bad universally. But it will be said, circumstances alter cases. It is good to tell the truth, but not the truth about the position of a merchant vessel to the commander of a hostile submarine. Be it so. It follows that truth-telling is not without further qualifications and conditions to be deemed good. Those justifications and conditions must be brought into the definition of the act before we deem it unambiguously good. What is unambiguously good is good universally. This axiom is essential to the rational character of moral judgments, and it was by insisting upon it above (Chapter I) that we established the principle of harmony. It is involved in the principle not strictly as a consequence, but rather as a logical condition of the principle itself. It follows (1) that what is unambiguously good for a person is good for every person; and (2) that if something good for one person is not good for another, the difference must rest upon a ground, and such ground must be some other good of universal character and applicability. This good might (*a*) be that of the person himself. What is good for *A* might be bad for B because B's personal requirements are different. Or (*b*) it might be that of some other person or persons, which happen to be in conflict with that which would really be for the good of B if it stood by itself. In this case our first principle refuses to allow any preference for A over B merely as one person against another. To assign a good to A and refuse it to B without further ground would be precisely the denial of any universal rule. But (1) the good in question might be much more important to A, or (2) others besides A might be involved and the good of many thus set against the good of one, or (3) the circumstances might be such that to satisfy A would accord with the common good while to satisfy B would conflict with it. Any of these considerations may be the foundations of universal rules justifying difference of treatment, with the proviso always that they take the good (or evil) to B into account, so that if circumstances are reversed it will be B who is to gain, while in any event the loss to him must be reduced to the smallest possible compass. These provisions, without which the rule of doing good and avoiding bad cannot be stated in universal terms, imply the equal con-

JUSTICE AND EQUALITY

sideration of A, B and all persons concerned in a transaction as finally determining the good of the transaction.

In the whole of this argument we are, I think, moving on ground antecedent to the principle of Harmony, or are drawing out more fully the implications on which it is based. In this way, as already hinted, equality is one of the premises on which Harmony is founded. But if now we advance to the principle, and assuming its correctness return upon the idea of equality which must be stateable in a form consistent with it, we get an important result. The conclusion reached above leaves us with the possibility of a final, theoretically irreducible, conflict between the good of one and the good of all. The principle of Harmony is opposed to any such conflict, and holds that acts and institutions are good not because they suit a majority, but because they make the nearest possible approach to a good shared by every single person whom they affect. On this principle that which is unambiguously good in each individual life is an internal harmony which is itself an element in a wider harmony of corresponding lives. Hence, the good of each cannot be finally determined without reference to the good of all who stand in mutual relations, i.e. the common good, and conversely in determining the comprehensive harmony the good of each is reckoned alike. In this ultimate sense equality of consideration is an essential element in the common good. Conversely, the conditions of harmony as between many people co-operating in divers ways entail diversities of behaviour and of treatment, and this is the sole and sufficient ground of differentiation.

All members of the community, then, simply as members have an equal claim upon the common good, while any difference in what is due to them or from them must itself be a difference required by the common good. It by no means follows that all claims are of equal strength. The claim of the individual may be for the conditions in which he can live in harmony with himself and his society. This is his real good, and its conditions his real need. It is clearly for the common good that such conditions should be satisfied, as the common good is simply the total of all the lives that are in mutual harmony. On the other hand, the claim of the individual may be for a mode of life which pleases him, but is not compatible with social service, and it is not for the common good that this claim should be sustained. The common good, therefore, supposes a differentiation between the conditions of social and those of an unsocial and imperfectly social life and personality, and is concerned to satisfy only the former which may be called in general the needs of its members.[1]

Needs differ in two ways. (*a*) To meet the same need, e.g. to satisfy his hunger one man needs more than another. In general terms the needs of human beings

---

[1] In more abstract terms the argument runs: According to the Principle of Harmony the object of moral endeavour is to establish and extend harmony and remove disharmony. Any person may have within him elements and capacities of harmony with others and also disharmony. What is inharmonious if it cannot be modified must be destroyed, but to repress or even to fail to stimulate and promote any element capable of harmonization is contrary to the moral purpose. This holds whatever, wherever, and in whomsoever the element may be. Thus, it is an impartial prin-

JUSTICE AND EQUALITY

are the same, viz. the conditions of full physical, mental, and spiritual development, and to the limits of its capacity it is the duty of the community to secure such conditions for every one of its members.* But the kind of "nurture" that the soul requires is not the same in all cases, and it may be asked whether it is the duty of the community to provide for the variations or only for the average. The answer is that even a single personality thwarted in a harmonious development of which it was capable is a loss to the common life. Given a real need, there is no question of the desirability of meeting it, but only of the adequacy of the common resources and of the judgment directing their application. (*b*) Needs differ in urgency. A certain minimum of food, clothing, etc., may be regarded as of absolute necessity. Certain additions to these add greatly to comfort and efficiency. Further additions have less effect. A law of diminishing returns applies pretty rigorously to the relations between healthy development and physical conditions. It is clear that the most urgent need is invariably to be preferred. Thus the minimum necessary to physical health and the normal growth of faculty takes precedence of all other personal claims, and in general so far as they

<hr />

ciple, irrespective of persons, according to which every man has a duty to and a claim upon every other, with whom he is in actual relation, in respect of the elements of potential harmony in his nature. The common good is the realized harmony of these elements in all members of the community, and its fundamental principles are those on which such realization is based. It fails— there is a wrong in it—if whatever harmony there be conflicts with an element of good in any member. Thus each man has a claim upon the common good proportioned to his own qualifications for sharing it. This is the fundamental principle of equality.

are distinguishable and classifiable necessaries take precedence of comforts, comforts of luxuries.[1] We may say then that there is an equal claim to equal needs.

Notwithstanding all these differences among needs, the principle of distribution by needs would be generally recognized as broadly a principle of equality. We have now to consider the ground of differentiation. Differences arise in a system in which all have a part, and a claim to equal consideration, from the necessities of the system itself. For example, captain and sailors have an equal interest in the safety of the ship, but for the sake of that safety such differences must be recognized as will ensure that the captain's orders will be carried out. In general terms, the common good is maintained by the services of its members, and is endangered or diminished by ill-behaviour. It is in turn bound to maintain all the functions which serve it, and restrain actions which harm it, and both requirements give rise to differential treatment. Every one of whom a given function is required may claim on his side the conditions necessary to its performance, e.g. if he has a certain political respon-

---

[1] It may be said that these distinctions are subjective. What is one man's luxury is another man's necessity. This is mainly due to social inequalities which have allowed some classes to become so accustomed to expensive modes of living that they would—at least for a time—find it a hardship to dispense with them. But this form of inequality has no social justification. There are also differences of temperament and physique independent of social institutions, which, e.g., make a mild narcotic like tobacco an extraordinary comfort to the average man, while not a few are indifferent or hostile to it. Differences of this sort are met by mere liberty. If a man has some margin above bare necessities he can make his own hierarchy of comforts and luxuries.

sibility he must be furnished with adequate powers. If he has to do hard and exacting muscular work, he must have food and rest in proportion. If he is a brain-worker he needs air and exercise to keep him fit. Thus different functions imply different special needs. Again, the restraint and ill-behaviour involves at lowest some restriction of personal liberty, which is a withdrawal of one of the general needs of personal development. The further discussion of these cases falls under the heads of economic and retributive justice respectively. For the moment we remark only that the equal claim to equal needs must be qualified by the necessity of adequate adjustment of conditions to functions, which have their various degrees of urgency in accordance with the nature of the need that they serve and of the difficulty of supplanting them with any alternative. It is clear that a function must not be too expensive, e.g. if it supplies a secondary need it must not cost so much as to hamper the supply of any primary needs. On the other hand, a function, however costly, is justified, if on the balance the community is better able to meet its needs with it than without it.

We may then define Distributive Justice as equal satisfaction of equal needs, subject to the adequate maintenance of useful functions. Bringing this definition to bear on the alternative meanings of equality set out above, we find that it selects as just the conception of equal satisfaction of equal needs, subject, however, to a condition prescribed by the needs themselves. This condition is the maintenance of the function upon which the common good depends, and this involves differential treatment of individuals in accordance with the nature of their services to the community. How far this squares with the conception of desert, whether the maintenance of functions would necessarily take the form of reward, and whether reward would go by effort or by performance, are questions which have yet to be examined. With regard to ill desert or misfunction, it emerges clearly from the definition that as functions of the common life are to be maintained, anything that obstructs them must be prevented, even at the cost of the withdrawal of some things that are in themselves good for those responsible for the obstruction, e.g. their liberty. How this bears on the theory of punishment will have to be considered further, but it is already clear that the good of the offender can never be left out of sight, and that he must suffer as little as is compatible with the good of others. With regard to special relations and special obligations arising out of them, it is clear that they will be admitted so far as they operate in a harmonious whole.

Before proceeding to the development of these matters, it will be well to consider certain difficulties and objections to the principle arrived at. To go at once to the root of the matter it may be maintained that though all individuals are doubtless entitled to some consideration, they are not even in the final analysis of the common good entitled to the same kind and degree of consideration. They are different beings, and the difference admits of a broad and general formulation. The capacity of any individual for the experience of good and evil is measured by his development. Now individuals vary very greatly in their actual development and even in their capacity of development. Admitting that if attainable it is a good thing that all should have opportunities for the development of which they are capable, it may be argued (1) that the lower development is of very little account in comparison with the higher, and that the perfect flower of a strong and rich soul is cheaply bought at the expense of further stunting some already poor and wan personality. The way of progress lies in strengthening the strong. The feeble capacity has its claim, but it is to count precisely for what it is worth and no more. If its interests can be reconciled with those of the stronger there is net gain, but if they cannot, if, that is, there is fuller development for the richer nature possible only through the loss of the weaker, then the weaker must suffer accordingly. Justice is that apportionment which will yield the greatest good; the greatest good lies in the fullest development; and if on the whole a fuller development can be reached by the crippling or extinction of some members of the community, they must be crippled or extinguished.

This argument, however, is on our principle false. It errs by taking development in the abstract instead of development in harmony as the measure of value, and thus arrives at the conclusion that one good—not accidentally or through the complication of individual circumstances, but essentially and universally—conflicts with another. This is contrary to our principle, and we must take it that whatever development of personality in a man is really admirable must be such as upon the whole tends not to the arrest but to the development of personality in others. No doubt we are unable to withhold admiration for great qualities in a man which are in fact working ill, but we are justified only in so far as such qualities suitably matched with others would in fact work well. The fascination exercised by Napoleon or Bismarck is an evidence of something slavish and cringing in human nature.

But (2) the argument, remodelling itself, may continue: "It is not a question of one personality against another, but of the common good and the collective achievement. In the end harmony—the harmony that is to be worth having, is to be won by a great exaltation of the power of man. It is the 'general deed' that counts, and the individual must go under. There would never have been organized industry without some sort of servile labour, never art or science without a leisured class. The subordination that produced these results was historically justified, and if we can get better results even now by similar, if milder, methods, they justify our use of them. We should deal as tenderly with the weak as the case admits, but we must not allow them to handicap us in the race." To all this again on the Principle of Harmony the reply has been indicated in Chapter II. The collective achievement that is desirable is just the sum of what is desirable for individuals when their interactions are taken into account. If there is collision between collective aims on the one side, and those aims which we should arrive at by an equal consideration of the well-being of all individuals on the other, then there is a disharmony, and we must go back on our data and revise our conclusions as we do in the case of a logical contra-

JUSTICE AND EQUALITY

diction.¹ But it may be said the collective aim is really justified in the future, and the present generation may have to sacrifice itself. There is eventual harmony, but—such being the hard conditions of life—attainable only by some disharmony now. If that is so, we should like to know when the harmony would begin. That an entire generation may have to put up with a certain loss for the sake of the future must be admitted, but it must be a vanishing loss of which we can see the end, and we may demand to see it with as much reasonable certainty as may be set against the positive certainty of the present sacrifice. The admission of some definite principle of disharmony into our social system is much too like the hospitality of the organism to a disease germ which is destined to multiply. At what point will inequality become unnecessary? At what point would the elimination or oppression of the weak by the strong cease to be arguable on the grounds here urged? Nations that change their constitution or make some fundamental alteration in their social system, such as the abolition of slavery in the British or of serfdom in the Russian empire, are wont to make some arrangements for a transition period in which the newly recognized right is but imperfectly applied. Such arrangements are only justi-

---

[1] We touch here on an antithesis between two principles which must be stated nakedly. If collective achievement is qualitatively distinct from and superior to personal achievement then the principle of Harmony fails, and equality along with it. If on the other hand the principle of Harmony is maintained, then collective achievement is the harmony of personal achievements carried to their highest power, and in this harmony every personality receives all the consideration which mutual consistency allows.

fied if they have their destined term, and that term must not be too long. On no other conditions could any refusal of equality be accepted in the principles of social organization.

As to the historical facts which are held to justify inequality by the test of success, they require careful reading in conjunction with clear discrimination between distinct meanings of the term before they are used for purposes of inference. It is true that the first advances in efficient social organization are made by tightening and enlarging authority, and, broadly, on the principle of subordination. It is further true that inequalities tend to increase with the enlargement of opportunity, and to crystallize themselves through inheritance. The very simplest societies know no differences of rank, no slavery, serfdom or caste. Even the headman or chief often stands little if at all above his followers. The development of class distinctions may be traced clearly in the uncivilized world by the constant increase in the percentage of peoples recognizing some form of slavery on the one hand, and of nobility on the other, as we pass from the Lower Hunters to the higher agricultural and pastoral groups.[1] (The archaic civilizations indicate a similar change.) Thus slavery is said to have been unknown in the early Chinese society. In the old Babylonian kingdom slaves were rare, in late Babylonian days they were numerous. The same may be said of Rome, and some districts of Greece like Phocis, which preserved much of their archaic structure, had no slaves in the

[1] See *The Material Culture and Social Institutions of the Simple Peoples*, by M. Ginsberg, L. T. Hobhouse, and G. C. Wheelerp.

classical period. We hear nothing of caste in the Vedas till we come to a single passage of late date. Both military and economic success make for inequality. The former in its cruder forms might take the shape of slave-raids as in the old kingdom of Egypt, or through systematic conquest might reduce all the original inhabitants to a lower status as in the Peloponnesus under the Dorians. Economic advance offers, in the first place, greater opportunities to men of ability, and inheritance perpetuates the resulting inequalities with cumulative effect. Hence it is that in modern times, in spite of a broad civic and political equality, we have contrasts of wealth and poverty which even opponents of abstract equality must recognize as a social danger.

Thus growing inequality is the automatic result of increased national power. But wherever the social conscience is alive its dangers have been seen. "Woe unto them that add house to house and field to field" say the Hebrew prophets, and their protests take effect in the Deuteronomic legislation. To save Athens, Solon had recourse to the desperate expedient of the Seisachtheia, yet two centuries later Plato declared that the city was two states in one territory divided against one another. The Gracchan legislation was a bold attempt to save the economic independence of the mass of citizens, and its eventual ill-success wrote the doom of the Republic. The only equality which the Roman world could secure was an indiscriminate subjection to the Imperial law. But with the Stoics the conception of Natural Equality came into being, and in Christianity it took the shape of a common brotherhood of all the sons of God. Starting from these foundations, modern law and ethics have, at any rate, insisted on the equal enjoyment of certain elementary rights, including among them the right of self-advancement. National, racial and sex prejudices find themselves confronted with a moral protest. The issue of the contest is not yet decided—and will not be until the ethical importance of equality is more clearly defined—but enough has been established to confute the easy view of the comfortable that inequality is inherent in progress. What is true is that the exercise of human power is the opportunity of higher faculty, and as the actual endowments of men are very various, social differentiation ensues. What moral criticism has to say is that the advantages so obtained may be won not only by useful but socially injurious qualities, that they may be used wisely and temperately, but also selfishly and oppressively, and that by the ubiquitous principle of inheritance they may be handed on to men who could never have won them for themselves or may be developed cumulatively generation by generation till they destroy the true unity of society. The equality of right which sets itself against these tendencies is no reversion to the undifferentiated primitive state. It is a feature of that highest and most vital civilization which, whether in ancient mediæval or modern times, has been the outcome of the civic principle, whether in the city or the so-called nation state. Differentiation is a necessary factor in all high organization, but the highest organization is not subordination under autocratic direction but the willing co-operation of free agents in a good which all enjoy. If it is argued that, as a brutal truth, civilized man has increased his stature by standing on the shoulders of others, it may be replied with confidence that every community resting on subordination has paid a heavy price for the contributions which its superior class may have made to the work of civilization, and that in general the greater responsibility put upon the strong and more capable to regard and serve the weaker, the keener is the stimulus to their faculties, and the purer and more human and more rational the law, the religion, the literature, the art and the philosophy which they evolve.

Hence in sum we cannot regard any partial development as good which is necessarily such as to obstruct development on corresponding lines in others. Nor can we regard any collective achievement as good which leads necessarily to the depression of individuals. There may be great inequalties of development, but to satisfy ethical requirements they may be such that the further the development is pushed in any one person, the more it tends on the whole to assist the corresponding development of all others whom it can affect. This is as much as to say that the rational good is one in which all persons share in proportion to the capacity of their social personality. This is the fundamental principle of proportionate equality in the Common Good, the governing conception of social justice.

To pass to a second objection: In principle all this, it may be said, is well enough, but it makes a gigantic assumption. It supposes that the material conditions of a good life for all are, in fact, at our disposal, if we choose to use them. But is this the case? It is at least so doubtful that we must contemplate the alternative position. Suppose, for example, that the resources of society only suffice to provide the conditions of a full development for some, and not for all. If the food will not "go round," which is better, that all should be weak and undeveloped, or that some should starve outright while others are healthy? To put the question more generally, is it not better that a good life should be attainable by some, though it is impossible for all? If Equality would mean a poor life for all while a carefully adjusted inequality would mean a good life for some, is not inequality a condition of the imperfect good that alone is in our power? Good or bad, we must first reply, it is certainly not just. Justice, we have seen, is in its essential principle founded on a good, common to all to whom it applies. The inequality suggested deliberately excludes from consideration the good of some of those to whom its rules apply. Whatever "good" there may be in social life on this foundation, it must limp along without the aid of justice. But let us consider whether there may not, after all, be some principles of justice applicable even under the conditions supposed. As it happens, the circumstances of war and blockade have brought all the nations of Europe sharply up against this question, and from their behaviour certain principles have emerged which I think may suggest an answer in general terms. (1) As long as it is a question not of actual starvation but of insufficiency, the rule has everywhere been that all should go short alike, with the significant exception that soldiers were as far as possible kept on full rations. Next to them came the men (or women) doing hard muscular work in the

JUSTICE AND EQUALITY

service of the armies. Thus each community, when fairly faced with the necessity of preserving the common life, resorted to equality subject to the maintenance of the most necessary common functions. (2) When, as in Russia and Austria, it became a question of actual starvation, the effort was made to preserve the children, and after them the aged and infirm, the latter as the more necessitous and dependent, the former also as the hope of the community, and as likely to suffer most from the temporary shortage. Here again we have (*a*) the ultimate service to the community, and (*b*) adjustment to needs, as the working principles. (3) If, finally, the point is reached at which either some must die or all must die, equality fails simply because it is no longer physically possible. On a torpedoed ship, if the last boat will only take twenty of the thirty that remain, it is better that twenty should be saved than that none should be saved. Justice can show itself only in the selection, and so far as they can men choose (1) those who can manage the boat (i.e. by function), (2) those who have the greatest claim on life, e.g. married people or mothers and children. In general, women and children are preferred partly because men (in accordance with a race-preserving instinct) place a higher value on their lives than on the lives of other men, partly because they are more helpless, and in preferring them the men have the compensation of death with honour. (3) The feeble generally. In their case a sentiment of justice operates, even if it be not easy to validate in its particular application, for, as a matter of justice, it is a general function of the strong to protect the weak, and though in the case contemplated weak and strong are much on a level, the sentiment holds, and is backed perhaps by the feeling that the strong have more endurance. Lastly, the preference for sharing death is one which it would be very unreasonable to impose,[1] but may very reasonably be felt and acted on by individuals, e.g. a husband and wife to whom death together appears quite clearly preferable to a life apart marred from the outset by a memory of a desertion.

Thus, not only in cases of deficiency, but even on occasions of emergency our principles hold as long as their application is physically possible, and the review of such cases suggests two riders of high importance in the doctrine of equality. The first is, that evil is lessened and good enhanced by sharing. The second is, that where necessaries are short, superfluities must vanish. No amount of unnecessary comfort is to be balanced against deprivation of necessaries in a single case. The comparison is not quantitative, as the common money measure delusively suggests, but qualitative. There is a difference in kind between the value of food to the hungry, and of turtle soup to the gourmet. If there is not difference in kind, there is vast difference in degree between the value of the simpler comforts and the more elaborate luxuries. The workman's pipe is worth more to him than the collection of rare gems to the millionaire. It is easily deduced that, unless in an enormously rich society, the social value of material wealth tends to increase as the

---

[1] If a climber who can no longer hold up his party declines to cut the rope and perfers to perish with them, that is due to the sense of solidarity to which the ethics of climbing and similar perilous adventures gives peculiar authority.

distribution becomes more equable. How far this tendency is offset by other circumstances we must inquire further in dealing with the economic aspect of justice.

CHAPTER VI

PERSONAL JUSTICE

JUSTICE, as we have seen, has to maintain the functions by which the needs of the community are served and to prevent misfunction or obstruction. What methods does it employ for this purpose? Is it a mere question of the most efficient means or is there a point of principle involved? The answer that will at once suggest itself is that the appropriate means of securing good service and preventing disservice is the familiar method of reward and punishment, and that this method is based not merely on its efficiency but on the principle of treating every man according to his deserts—giving him that to which he is morally entitled. To find and assign to moral desert its due seems the very kernel of the problem of justice.

Yet the analysis of desert presents great difficulties. For example, to begin with a question already touched, does it rest on effort or on performance? Are the deserts of the honest and industrious, but incompetent man, the same as those of the efficient? If we say No, we give the efficient credit to which he does not seem morally entitled. We reward him for the qualities which he does not create but finds within himself, as much a gift of fortune as inherited rank or wealth. If we say Yes, we compel society to put the same value upon ability and stupidity, strength and weakness, failure and success, and to go no further—that hardly seems just to those who have to pay for them. And we may raise this further question. The denial of merit to capacity, to success as such, implies that desert pertains to the moral will alone. But if we go far enough back, is the moral will itself something which a man makes for himself any more than he makes his intellectual capacity? No doubt he develops it by usage, but does he not develop his intellect, or any other capacity in the same way? The will at bottom is a synthesis of elementary tendencies, and if A as he grows up develops a good and B a bad will, does not this in the end mean that A and B differ either in their circumstances or in their original endowment and so in their dealings with circumstances—in either case in points for which not A and B but whatever forces fashioned them and their lives were "responsible"?

Thus the question of desert pushes us into the problem of responsibility, and if by responsibility we mean the ultimate causation of some result, good or bad, we shall hardly find any means of fixing it within an unending stream of causation. If, however, responsibility means the operation of a causal process of a particular kind, without reference to the antecedents which brought that process into being, we may be able to deal with it. Now a responsible agent is one who knows what he is about, no matter how he came to know, or came to be disposed to one course or another. As responsible, he is knowingly directing his action to some end because that end appeals to him. His action is in fact determined in detail and as an entire plan by its bearing upon the end, and it is this which differentiates the causal action of an intelligent responsible being from that of an inanimate or an unintelligent being. Nor does responsibility cease when the act is over. As the effects develop, the intelligent being can look back just as he could look forward and attribute them to his own act as the initiatory step, and it is not always until he does this that he can realize precisely what he has done. The action does not look the same in retrospect as in prospect, and it is by means of the comparison that he educates his will. Now will is the central function of the active life, organizing, shaping and co-ordinating all other functions, and if it is the sense of responsibility which maintains and develops the will, it is clear that responsibility has an essential function in the active life. It is also clear that responsibility is confined to the sphere of will. It does not matter how the will originally came to be, any more than it matters how other qualities came to be. What matters is that voluntary action is responsible action, action determined by relation to its ends as these are appreciated or understood, and modifiable by an improved appreciation.

The natural education and discipline of the will, then, lies in each man's realizing the consequences of his voluntary acts. Now realizing them means not merely knowing, intellectually, what they are, but feeling them, since it is ultimately feeling which guides the will. It is the sense of this discipline which lies at the root of retributive justice. The fruits of his voluntary act are the man's moral deserts, but it is in fact generally impossible that he and he alone should bear the whole of them, since, whether for good or evil, the most significant acts have the widest and deepest social effects. The pure retributive theory which makes a man the sole bearer of the consequences of his acts implies a quite impossible individualism. Expiation, often desired by the offender himself, is a mystical manner of making believe to overcome the difficulty. By taking the consequences on his own head the offender may, at least, avert from others the wrath of the gods, or the evil operation of curses and taboos which have been set going. If the realities of life could be so dealt with, expiation would be the true principle of punishment,[1] and that is why the idea still holds with us, though we know that the real consequences of action cannot be thus distorted. Just as expiation implies an impossible individualism, so the conception of virtue as its own sufficient reward, and vice as its own sufficient punishment, implies an impossible socialism. If and in so far as we already identify ourselves with the common good we doubtless feel the good or evil of our acts in the same moment as we perceive them. But if we always felt like that we should be always automatically doing our best. In reality we all have interests—and not merely low and selfish, but quite legitimate interests, including our feeling for those near to us—which are not necessarily identical with the common good. Paradoxically enough, it is for the common good that we should have such interests, since the common good in the end does not lie in the suppression but in the exaltation of the personal life.

[1] Within limits touched on below, pp. 144-5.

What the common good requires of us is that in pursuance of these interests we should be governed by certain principles of universal application. Now to realize—that is, at once to understand and feel—the bearing of our actions on the common good is the true ethical discipline of the will.

This discipline is the main social function of retributive justice which seeks by a mechanism of rewards and punishments to make each man share in the fruits of his action and bring home to him what he has done. But though this is its main function, I do not think that it is the ultimate root of retributive justice. This root is traceable directly to the Principle of Harmony and its corollary the equal partnership in rights and duties. For we may consider retribution first as something due *to* the individual and, secondly, as something due *from* society. In the first relation we carry the appeal, if necessary, from the laws and practices of men to God, the Universe, the nature of things. We are outraged if the good man perishes while the wicked flourishes like a green bay tree. On the first count we are in the right, for it is the good man and he alone who is really capable of enjoying harmony and happiness, and when his life is marred the principle of harmony is defeated. On the second count, our case is not so clear, for, to begin with, the bad man is the victim of internal disharmony which really prevents him from enjoying the advantages which seem to be his unfair reward, and to proceed, if we may justly resent the waste of good things on one who only makes a bad use of them, are we justified in wishing him —as the natural man in us does wish him—an increment of evil? Let us defer this question for a moment and pursue the case of reward. We see the reasonableness of wishing all the conditions of happiness to him who is fitted to enjoy them, but might it not be said that here our duty ends? This natural harmony is its own reward, and if we introduce any extraneous consideration we only mar the purity of motive. But this argument overlooks the true relation of the common and the private good. The private is not merged in the common, but sustained and developed (however much modified) within it. It is in general desirable that each man should have his private circle of interests and should be able to enlarge it. At the same time it is essential that the private and the common should be harmonized, and that is secured if in serving the common good a man also serves his own. It is not a question of motive. The more unselfish this is, the more should the community on its side take care that so far as possible its faithful servant should be no loser.

We have already laid down that justice required the adequate maintenance of functions. So much appeared from the bare consideration of the needs of the community. Our present result may be considered as the further definition of the term "adequate." To be adequate to the requirements of justice there must be such reciprocity between the community and its servant as harmonizes the private and common interest, and this is the function of reward. It is clear that the reward must be sufficient to maintain the function in the sense of repaying the individual what it costs him (e.g. in physical energy). Whether it is anything more than this and how it is adjusted to the several constituents of desert will be considered in the field in which the question is really important—that of economic justice.

We turn back to the more difficult question of punishment. Let us first ask whether we can definitely and justifiably wish evil to a bad man. To the question put nakedly, few will answer in the affirmative. They will ride off it by declaring punishment to be a good in disguise. This is to commit themselves to the reformatory theory and the consequence that, if reform can be accomplished by pleasant methods without suffering, that will suffice. The implication is that the infliction of suffering or other evil is not an ethical necessity. We are not greatly helped if for "inflicting" evil we substitute "sharing" evil, for partnership in evil is not the same thing as partnership in good. If, indeed, the evil is lightened by sharing, as it often is, that is a reasonable consideration, but if it is a question of adding to it by the infliction of further suffering, that merely brings us back to the first position. It may be said that at any rate the evil ought to fall as far as possible on the offender, and that if he has any redeeming sense of guilt that will be his own desire. This view is in fact the foundation of the expiatory theory of punishment and has its place where the consequences of wrong-doing are conceived as spiritual or magical in character. The offender then—perhaps of his own goodwill—takes on his own head the wrath of the offended god, or the dread efficacy of the broken taboo, and so redeems himself and saves society. With us it is clear that expiation can only have a limited application and a kind of symbolic significance. We can understand its appeal, but it cannot avert the invariable consequences of the deed that is done. Behind this is the question whether after all it is quite just. We are all miserable sinners, so that the offender is one of ourselves. How much evil would we have fall upon him? Would we concentrate all the lightnings upon him to his utter destruction, or would we, after all, draw some of them to ourselves so that the strokes, breaking on a greater surface, may be less deadly? This seems the course indicated by the sense of fellowship, and if so, it limits expiation to the degree or kind of suffering required by the sense of responsibility, and brings us back once again to reform and re-constitution of character.

It seems, then, that we cannot rightly wish evil as such, that is any kind of evil, merely because it is evil, to the offender. Yet there is a form of suffering which is inherent in the repair of the broken ethical order, the suffering involved in the realization by the offender of the thing that he has done. This we rightly and reasonably wish him, for we want him to enter into the ethical community as a conscious and responsible agent, and I think that it is the desire for such realization which is the ethical kernel of the commonplace indignation which expresses itself in gross punishments. This seems to me the one and only form of punishment which is in itself desirable. Punishment as a means is quite a different matter. Society has a right and a duty to protect itself, and may do so not only by restraint upon the criminal, but also by menace. Terror is the lowest and worst of all possible motives, but before we think we can dispense with it, let us reflect on the number of quite respectable people who are only deterred from minor breaches of police regulations by the fear of fines and other inconveniences. It would, I fear, be useless to prescribe that all bicycles should carry a rear lamp without prescribing a fine for the delinquent. The punishment which we inflict must be so conceived as to do the least harm and the most good to the offender compatible with its efficiency as a menace—for the offender is one of ourselves and we must wish him good so far as it stands in with the common good. But I gravely doubt whether we ought to punish adults from the motive of reform alone. Punishment is itself to the adult so degrading, that the best we can ordinarily hope for is some compensating good, and if the punishment is not required for our protection I think we should leave him to wrestle matters out with his own conscience and the opinion of his neighbours.

In fine, the only punishment which is desirable in itself is an inward and spiritual process which society cannot ensure. Its reaction on the criminal is justified only as a means to its own safety, and even so, must have the good and not the evil of the criminal in view so far as the condition of this safety allows. It remains wrong to wish any avoidable extension of evil, while to inflict it for the good of the offender is an inversion of the true order of motive. The good of the offender should palliate or modify the shape and form of the evil inflicted for the good of society. Thus, in the inward sense as something due to the individual "at the hand of God" punishment is, like reward, an integral part of the ethical order. In the outward sense as something due from society it is not, like reward, a part of ideal justice, it is a mechanical

PERSONAL JUSTICE 147

and dangerous means of protection which it requires the greatest wisdom and humanity to convert into an agency of reform.

Upon the whole then, the view which sees desert at the core of justice is not far out. The fundamental of justice is the universality of the system of harmony. Harmony must extend to all to whom it can extend, and that includes all men of good will. From this follows the rule that good service calls for co-operation, reciprocity, and the harmonization of the private with the common good. This is the function of reward. On the other hand bad will is of itself excluded from harmony except under conditions of painful re-education which constitute its necessary punishment. But the infliction of further suffering is not intrinsically desirable. It is a mechanical means of protecting society, intrinsically an undesirable means, to be purged as far as possible by the consideration of the good of the offender. Thus, when we translate the conception of desert into the working code of society we find that it justifies and develops that part of our first principle which insisted on the adequate maintenance of useful functions and by consequence and contrast, the arrest of misfunctions. This is the application we have to make of desert. There is an inner sphere in which it operates of itself.

A traditional view of the subdivision of justice would suggest that in the last chapter we were dealing with distributive justice and in the present with Corrective, or perhaps Retributive Justice, while in the projected account of economic reward in the next chapter we shall be engaged in Commutative Justice. It is not, however, easy to carry through these or any subdivisions without over-lapping. Distributive justice means an apportionment as between members of a community, and in this both reward and punishment—functions of retributive justice—play a part. I think that in the last chapter what we really dealt with was justice as considered from the point of view of needs, for we urged the equal needs of all members qualified by the maintenance of functions which we then regarded purely as a need of the community. As implying both equality of sharing and unity of collective interest the term "communal" is sufficiently suited to designate the principles of justice so arrived at. In the present chapter we have clearly been treating justice more from the personal point of view. This has had the effect of further defining one clause in our definition of communal justice. The next chapter will apply this definition in the special sphere of economics.

CHAPTER VII

THE PAYMENT OF SERVICE

REWARD, we have seen, is a function of harmony. On what principles is harmonization to be effected? In many departments of life the simple principle that good service requires the conditions appropriate for maintaining it is a sufficient guide. For example, capacity demands the power and responsibility by which alone it can be displayed. But in the realm of economics this principle needs development and criticism. Here quantitative apportionment becomes a very important question, and its principles need a more elaborate discussion. We are dealing here with mutual service wherein what each man gives may be regarded indifferently as his service to the other, or the reward for the other's service to him. Now, in any economic system the maintenance of functions involves such exchange, for though a rigid socialistic system might supersede and suppress buying and selling, it would still demand of the individual certain services, and would give him in return a maintenance, which would not in general consist of what he makes or does, but would be a fraction of a total to which many contribute. All economic collaboration, voluntary or involuntary, direct or indirect, involves a transmutation of the product of the individual into a share of the products of other individuals. What is the rule of justice in this transmutation? At first sight any one would say that the simple rule of justice in exchange is that values given and taken should be equal, but axiomatic as this may appear it is necessary to examine it closely in relation to our principles. In exchange two parties perform a function in respect of each other, and their interests must accordingly be harmonized. This implies that both benefit by the transaction, and that one does not benefit in any respect by the other's loss. What is the proof that the exchange satisfies these conditions? First we may apply the subjective test of the willing transaction. The two parties will not willingly exchange unless both anticipate a benefit. But this is a doubtful test. For example, one party, though in the end he consents to the bargain, may do so only under the pressure of severe need, and the other party may be exposed to censure for taking undue advantage. Again, either party may act on insufficient information, and afterwards find out his mistake. We pass judgments on such transactions, which seem to indicate that we always have in mind some more objective standard of fairness, that is to say, we think of things as having a value which they should command. Now there is an existent standard of value for a thing if there is a general power of freely exchanging it against other things. Its power to purchase any one of the things of a class or multiples or fractions of other things is its exchange value. This general power to purchase determines what it is just to receive from a particular man. For if equal values are taken and given there is no loss, since each party obtains what he could

THE PAYMENT OF SERVICE

have replaced by the same third thing, and there is benefit, since each obtains the particular thing for which he happens to have most use. If, on the other hand, either party gets more than the exchange value, he benefits by the loss to the other of so much purchasing power.

Thus exchange at equal values is just if we consider it as an isolated transaction in an open market where values are determinate and all sorts of exchanges readily made. But in fact exchange is not an isolated transaction but a link in a series, and if we want to know whether the whole series is working fairly and whether the system which governs it is a just one we must look at the standard of value itself. We then find sometimes that the standard is uncertain, as, e.g., if the use-value of a thing depends much on individual circumstances, or if prices are exposed to fluctuation. For example, a man sells something for £5 as the market price of to-day, but owing to fluctuations of the standard it may have cost him £2 or £5 or £10 to bring to market. The transaction by itself under the circumstances of the day is just, but the whole series to which it belongs works out very differently to the seller in the cases supposed, and if he is in the event a loser through circumstances which he could not control there is a disharmony somewhere, and therefore an injustice, though it may be difficult to locate and impossible to impute to any particular person. Again, the article which he sells at £5 may be the product of much labour, involving high vital cost to A, while the money may have been come by easily by B. Again we can impute no injustice to B, but we surmise something wrong in the standard of value. In short, exchange is in incident in the production and distribution of wealth, and must be judged by its bearing on the whole of these processes.

From what has been said it will be apparent that in the economic field justice will be achieved by exchange at equal values provided that the standard of value is fixed by justice in general. Now the general principles of justice as laid down above are that there shall be equal provision for equal needs subject to the adequate maintenance of the functions by which such needs are supplied, and this latter clause was further defined as covering the harmonization of the private interests of the performer of the function with those of the community. These are the principles of just economic organization to which the standard of value must be accommodated. Let us see how they apply.

The first consequence is that the general economy should be directed to meeting the needs of all members of the community in proportion to their urgency, but always in such manner and under such conditions as to maintain the necessary economic functions. So far as the productive workers are concerned, we have seen that the just method of maintaining their functions is by securing to them suitable conditions for their work and harmonizing their interests with those of the community through remuneration. The principles of remuneration will be discussed presently. But there are also non-productive classes whose needs have to be met though they make no return for them, e.g. children, the aged, the disabled, the permanently defective, the wastrel, and the criminal. The first four classes have a moral claim on us for the best that we can afford. The wastrel and the

THE PAYMENT OF SERVICE 153

criminal have claims to such treatment as, however deterrent it may be, will not tend to their further deterioration, as, e.g., by insufficient feeding and bad housing. But subject to these considerations, the provision of needs without equivalent service in return must be so determined in amount, and more particularly in form, as to lay no crippling burden on production and offer no encouragement to idleness. Need simply as need is a claim, but not a completely validated claim till its bearing on function has been considered. This bearing at the points where difficulties of principle appear will be considered in its place.

The second consequence is that, apart from such common provision for needs as is made on the above conditions,[1] there is no method of acquiring wealth except by social service. There is no functionless wealth and no opportunity of earning income by socially useless or injurious work.

The third consequence is that the lowest remuneration

[1] I do not say "apart from provision for the helpless, etc.," because it may be convenient to supply certain needs quite unconditionally, e.g. we supply the use of roads, open spaces, and main drainage without charge. We also supply education to a point gratuitously. It might be deemed desirable to extend such supply to other cases, for reasons which need not be entered into here. It is sufficient that all needs supplied without return would be either (a) special to the classes above mentioned, or (b) universal for all members of the community, and in either case are governed by their bearing on the performance of economic functions. Thus a claim on wealth may rest on a need and then is valued under the conditions indicated for every one experiencing that need whose case conforms to the conditions. Or it may rest upon a function and then is valid for every one who performs that function. But it cannot rest on any other ground.

for work done is that which will maintain the least capable worker not employed from charity but actually required by the operation of the industrial system in a condition of full civic efficiency, that is to say not only in health but in a position to develop and exercise his faculties, to enter upon marriage and parenthood, and meet whatever costs of a normal family are not undertaken by the community. This is the lowest standard required to harmonize the interests of the worker and the community, for without it the producer does not secure the elementary and essential conditions of a good life.

Two criticisms may be passed on this doctrine. One is that the least skilled cannot earn the minimum. The community may conceivably give it them out of the surplus produced by other men if that suffices. But they cannot give equivalent value for it. The real value of their work is measured by their actual earnings in a system of free exchange, and in such a system unless the position of labour is exceptionally fortunate, as in a new and rich country, we do not find that unskilled earnings reach the civic minimum. By various devices, trade unionism, wages boards, etc., we may attempt to raise them to such a minimum; but even supposing (what is in doubt) that we can be permanently successful in so doing, we are still in reality giving the better wage, and it is not being earned. The reply is that in a competitive system what an individual can earn depends not only on his power of work, but on his power of getting himself paid for it. The second point is partly a matter of personal qualifications, though not of those qualifications which are socially most valuable. It is, however, mainly dependent on social conditions, which so operate that the poorer a man is the less in general is his chance of escaping from poverty. Now a just system differs from a competitive system in eliminating this second condition and substituting its own standard of remuneration, which is so conceived as to harmonize the interests of the producer and the community. From the point of view of the producer the governing principle of the harmony is that the lowest remuneration must yield the civic minimum. From the point of view of the community the weakest worker must be able to produce so much that when he is paid the community is not poorer. That is to say, he is the weakest worker who is required, not of charity, by the working of the system. This fixes the minimum standard of the remuneration of work in a justly ordered system, and it is clear that in such a system the weakest worker is earning his pay.

The real questions that arise here are two. The first is one of fact. What proportion of possible workers would this system exclude? Every increase of wages threatens to exclude a certain number of workers. But experience shows that ordinarily the number excluded is in the end very small if not nil. For over several generations substantial increases of real wages have taken place, and there is no evidence of permanent increase of unemployment. The reason is that the better remuneration of the worker not only improves his personal efficiency and that of his children, but also modifies the industrial organization. In a system which is still in the main competitive, it eliminates the methods which only pay with low wages and substitutes higher organization. It causes, as we might expect, a certain shifting of values all through the productive system, and a general increase of production.[1]

The second question is one of right. Beyond bare necessities the civic minimum is not absolutely rigid, and it must be admitted that in a poor community it cannot

[1] The probable effects of attempts to establish a "living wage" have recently been very fully and impartially examined by Professor Pigou (*Economics of Welfare*, Pt. III, chaps. vi–xvii). To discuss his arguments at all adequately would require a separate volume. I confine myself to a remark on one statement which I take to be his central assumption. "When things have settled down in more or less stable conditions, the play of economic forces tends to secure that in industries in general wages do correspond to the marginal net product of labour" (p. 538). On this two comments here must suffice: (1) This is at most only a tendency, obstructed by a variety of causes clearly set out by Professor Pigou. In consequence, there always exists a mass of exploitation (i.e. payment below the value of the marginal net product). If exploitation is constantly being eliminated by transference of labour it is constantly renewed by every weak bargainer thrown on the industrial market. If it can be eliminated the general average of wages will be permanently raised, and a number (though not necessarily an assignable class) of workers will find their position improved. This is the primary object of the impartial settlement of wages. (2) The marginal net product of labour depends on the quality and quantity of the labour available, on the standard of organizing ability among employers, on the direction given to that ability, and on the proportions in which labour-costs enters into prices. These things, as Professor Pigou's discussion sufficiently shows, are materially affected by wage regulations. Not only may a temporary increase of wages react on the efficiency of the worker, and through the family life on his children, but they affect the employer and the industry. They eliminate the employer who is enabled to muddle along with bad appliances because he can get labour cheap, as well as the type of employer whose efficiency consists in his power of "driving" his men. In consequence, they tend to select for the class of employers (and here the term may include managers, assistants and foremen) men who under-

be raised as high as in a rich one.[1] The attempt to do so would be found to eliminate a substantial proportion from the wage-earning system, and the community would carry a larger burden of dependants. With regard to secondary needs—comforts—there is then a certain allowable elasticity, but a justly ordered community will keep its minimum at the highest point at which it is permanently possible to secure employment for all who are not palpably defective.[2]

---

stand how to make the best of their workers and to make good wages pay. In the same way they tend to eliminate industries in places and in forms in which they are doing badly and transfer their custom to those better equipped. In all these ways the marginal net product of labour is affected, and if this is in fact the equilibrium point to which wages tend, then it must be said that the regulation of wages, if impartial and judicious, may set up a new equilibrium point, while also by reducing exploitation effecting a closer adjustment of actual wages to this point. Professor Pigou (op. cit. p. 542) is right in distinguishing a "living wage" from a "living income." But I think he goes too far when he says that "the enforcement in any industry of a living wage, in any plausible sense of that term, would go a very little way towards ensuring a "living income" even to those workpeople who regularly received it. A "living wage" is surely one calculated to suffice as a living income for the majority, and if it were universally enforced the necessity of additions in order to make a "living income" would be the exception, while if only a minority obtained the living wage it would be the rule.

[1] Cf. Pigou, Part V, chap. xii, cap. p. 790.

[2] The theoretical difficulty here is to measure defect. There are physical and mental defectives about whom there is no doubt. Between them and the normal unskilled worker there is a fringe of uncertain dimensions consisting (1) of the elderly—and in some cases age begins to tell after fifty, (2) of those partially disqualified by disease or accident, (3) of those with no definite disqualification but simply stupid or slow workers. It is not desirable to cast off

The principle of the civic minimum wage is, however, open to criticism from another point of view. The prime needs of all must be met without regard to their work simply because they are prime needs. Even the criminal must be kept in bodily health, and the child who is not an earner must be secured the education which will give him the chance of developing his faculties. It is therefore, it may be said, something of a mockery to tell the unskilled worker that he is earning what he would in any case receive from the community for his needs as a human being.

any of these from all employment, but to bring them up to the civic minimum is impracticable. They constitute an intermediate class not fully required by industry which could dispense with them with little or no loss, and yet capable of working and benefiting by so doing. In practice the Trade Boards have dealt successfully with this class by means of the permit system which allows them to be exempted from the minimum rates on such conditions as the Board may impose. In practice this means that their employer offers a reduced rate, which is carefully considered by the Board advised by an investigating officer or by one or more of its own members who visit the firm and see the worker. The Board makes its estimate of the deduction which the defect might be expected to make from the value of the worker as compared with the man or woman who is willingly employed at the general minimum rate and issues its permit accordingly. Being administered by employers and workers who know the conditions from both sides and have a common interest—the rates being once fixed—in seeing that they are not undermined, the system works well and secures a minimum rate for ninety to ninety-five per cent of the workers without inflicting avoidable hardship on the residue. Under the existing Acts "slow-workers" as such cannot be exempted. It was feared that this designation was too vague and would undermine the rates. After considerable experience in working the system I should feel no apprehension under this head. The Board ought to fix a rate which is as near the civic minimum

The answer to this is first that what a man earns he receives as his true and full property with unlimited right of disposal. What the helpless, the defective, the idler receive they receive as an allowance for the specific purpose of meeting their needs at the judgment of the community, and in such form and under such conditions as the community think fit to prescribe having regard to the effect on the general maintenance of economic functions.[1] They are dependants. Even if they receive as the circumstances of the industry permit. All the workers whom the trade definitely requires will be able to earn it. There will be a fringe whom the trade can absorb at a lower rate, and it is better for them to earn what they can than to be wholly dependent. What their disqualification is does not in principle matter. It is a question of administration. With regard to the elderly, who form the largest class, it may be pointed out that the true living minimum is lower, as in general they have no longer any family responsibilities. Permits are very freely given to workers over sixty-five, and it is a question of administration rather than principle whether lower minimum rates might be applicable to advanced years. One qualification should, however, be subjoined. The subnormal worker must not be a loser by his work as compared with the wholly dependent. His needs must be made good up to the civic standard, and if his disqualification is not one affecting parenthood, the standard should be that which provides for the duties of married life.

[1] It is, however, clear that the whole of our argument substitutes the alternative right to labour or maintenance. Moreover, the maintenance of intermittent labour cannot justly be regarded as involving dependence. It is the fault of bad industrial organization that reserves of labour often left unemployed are requisite. On our principle all labour that is positively required by the working of the economic system is entitled to the full reimbursement of its vital cost, and unfortunately this vital cost extends with but little diminution over the periods of idleness. To ignore them is to treat the worker as a machine which can run or stand still as required without deterioration, and such treatment is the direct contrary of elementary justice in economics.

a money allowance their expenditure may be so far supervised that, if they waste it, it may be withdrawn and institutional provision substituted. The money is given them for a purpose, and not theirs in absolute ownership. Hence even if they received as much as the earner it would not be under the same conditions. Further, while the helpless are a charge upon the humanity of the community, they have not an unqualified right to burden the community with their children, and maintenance in their case means maintenance of an individual apart from the responsibilities of parenthood and marriage.[1]

The fourth consequence is that every increase of effort, whether due to the arduousness of the work or the increased application of the worker, involves an additional human cost and earns justly a proportionate reward.

---

[1] Those who would solve the wages problem by the endowment of motherhood do not seem to pay much attention to the difference between maintenance and earnings. If the State maintains wife and children it will undoubtedly claim to govern marriage, parenthood, and the domestic economy. Some may think that a good thing. I do not propose to argue the point here, but merely to draw attention to the consequence. In the present connection I content myself with this proposition. The governing need of a good economic system is that it should provide for the humblest workers that it uses the financial wherewithal of full civic efficiency, including therein the power of maintaining a normal family in all those necessaries which the State does not supply. What the State will do well to supply and what to leave to the parent may be considered in another connection. But one implication is clear, that as long as the mother keeps the house a man's minimum wage must be computed on the basis of the needs of a normal family. The alleged consequence of injustice to women workers is imaginary, as will appear later.

Just remuneration must suffer to cover all vital costs. In making up the account we must moreover allow for the costs of training, and this will in general put the more skilled work on a higher basis than the less skilled.

But with the comparison of degrees of skill, including brain work, we come upon our real difficulty. Are we to go mainly by vital cost, i.e. effort, or by result? It is by no means clear that human costs increase in proportion to the social value of the nature of the work. Intellectual work and responsible work are certainly taxing, but probably less taxing than coal-mining, or even than agricultural work that involves constant exposure to all weathers. Hence, if we keep to remuneration based on vital cost, we do nothing to reorganize the greater social value of high-grade work. It may, indeed, be pointed out—it often is pointed out—that the actual recognition of such work in any known economic system is of the most uneven kind. The best social work is unpaid and unpayable, and it is only the talent which in addition to being useful is also marketable that gets its proportionate reward. But that consideration does not solve our problem. We want to know what is just, i.e. whether it is desirable to reward valuable service in proportion to its value, and not only to its cost to the worker. Here a well-known theory of remuneration suggests itself, which is in some sort the antithesis to that which we have so far assumed. This is the theory that the producer is entitled to the whole of his product, and therefore in an exchange system to its total value. Now, on examination it will be seen that the second clause of this theory does not follow simply and straightforwardly from the first. If I pick blackberries on an open common it may be fairly maintained that in the absence of any special obligation to the contrary, I am entitled to all the blackberries that I pick. But if I pick the blackberries to sell, then their price is a function of other variables than the amount and quality of my own picking. It depends on the amount put upon the market by other pickers, on the alternatives to blackberries for jam-making, and on the amount of money (and sugar!) which housewives have available. That is to say, it depends on widely ramifying social factors. If we proceed to higher and more complicated forms of production, the social factor penetrates the process more and more. I plough the land, but not with a plough which I made myself, to say nothing of inventing it myself. The organizer of industry who thinks that he has "made" himself and his business has found a whole social system ready to his hand in skilled workers, machinery, a market, peace and order—a vast apparatus and a pervasive atmosphere, the joint creation of millions of men and scores of generations. Take away the whole social factor and we have not Robinson Crusoe, with his salvage from the wreck and his acquired knowledge, but the naked savage living on roots, berries and vermin. *Nudus intravi* should be the text over the bed of the successful man, and he might add *sine sociis nudus exirem*. What can justly be said is not that A of his own efforts creates so much wealth and B so much, but that operating on and with the existing social system the increment of wealth due to A is greater or less by so much than that due to B. Now, if the account were between A and B alone, that might conceivably determine the basis of remuneration; but in the account between A or B and Society it fails because the co-operating society is the major factor in both cases. A and B will exchange at equal values of their produce, but what we want to know is the standard which determines these values. This standard must secure to A and B a measure of remuneration which will harmonize their respective interests with the common good.

On this basis it may be argued that sufficient provision has already been made by the principles laid down. A and B perform functions which entail a certain vital cost. We meet this adequately, and the function is accordingly maintained. Each must do his best as a matter of social duty, and if it costs A no more to give us the fine fruits of his intellect than it costs B to yield his hard dull toil, then we must leave it at that. To this stoical conclusion, however, two answers suggest themselves: (1) As a matter of psychology should we get the best out of our best men in this way? As to this, the answer is not simple and unambiguous. So far as the very best men are concerned, it is probably an affirmative. All they ask is the provision of the needs of their toil, the instruments, the opportunities, the necessary powers and they give their work as a labour of love. Of the majority, who are not altogether of this type, it is not possible to speak in universal terms. The value of reward, and in particular of profit as a motive, has been immensely exaggerated. Those with whom it is the sole motive are, perhaps, as rare as those with whom it is no motive at all. But it takes all sorts to make a world. Indirect results of high remuneration, dignity, or the leisure and freedom to be won, are powerful inducements to some. To others recognition means a great deal, and when it is withheld they suffer a dull resentment. Then again there is the adventurous type, attracted by high prizes and unwilling to respond with its greatest effort unless to such a stimulus, and at the other end of the character scale the plodder and saver, who will undertake the long preparatory period of the professions, looking forward to a constant accession of relative ease and comfort. Upon the whole, there is little doubt that if we take human nature as it is—and it is really useless to take it as it is not—some measure of remuneration by achievement as distinct from effort does directly or indirectly promote achievement. (2) But we have still to ask whether such differentiation is just in the sense that it is an intrinsically desirable element in a social system, or only necessary in the sense that it is the price which the more capable can demand of us for their services. Here, then, is our second answer. The common good is not something outside the good of A and B, but inclusive of their personal interests so far as these are harmonizable with those of C and D and the rest. Each man has his own life and his own circle, which, under the said conditions, it is desirable for him to enjoy. One of his needs, that is to say, is liberty, scope, opportunity, and our system will be the better the fuller the opportunity that it yields him. Now, may we not say, so far as economic relations are concerned, that society owes to a man not only the opportunity of useful service, but also the opportunity of making the most of himself and his own life

THE PAYMENT OF SERVICE

in his own way, provided that he gives fair value for all that he enjoys, and he gives fair value provided that, however much he himself may be enriched by his efforts, society also is enriched by them. Society, that is, owes him the chance of improving his own position by his talents on the condition that their use is such as at the same time to serve society.[1] Once more the protest may be, he ought of his own free will to give his best to society without reward. But does not the point of this protest lie in the words "free will"? Could it with the same force be maintained that society may rightly compel him to that service, or would this not look rather like a kind of sweating of talent? If so—and notwithstanding the force of the opposite argument the balance seems to be

---

[1] A friendly critic points out that the principle still leaves an indeterminate margin. For though the rate of remuneration must be such that each addition to the producer's income is won by a service which has positive net value to society after the additional remuneration is paid, there is nothing to show what the proportion between the two sums is to be. The producer might take the bulk of the increment, leaving only a small margin to society or *vice versa*. Is there any principle on which the proportion can be justly determined? It is not enough for our purpose to reply that it will always be wise to make the payment demanded as long as society secures a net gain, however small, for we are not asking about a necessity which it is wise to admit but about a rule of justice upon which the community and the individual may agree. On this basis the only reply seems to run on the lines suggested below (p. 169) that the rates of increment which satisfy average human desire and thus in general supply a sufficient incentive to the great majority of men are justly applicable to all cases. We may have to pay more than this as the monopoly price of high ability, but if so we pay of compulsion, not of justice. (See also the further qualification as to large incomes indicated below, loc. cit.).

on this side—we must admit achievement or utility of work done as a ground of remuneration in supplement to effort and the compensation of vital cost.

The issue is in part dependent on the character of the particular community. If the antithesis were simply and straightforwardly between private and common interests, if, that is to say, the best and ablest men could have confidence that whatever wealth their talents produce, if it does not come to them would fall into the hands of a wise power which would apply it to the best human purposes, they might well be content to ask nothing but so much as would sustain them in the performance of their function. If, on the other hand, common wealth is to be administered by a rather stupid and commonplace State, and three-fourths of it used for armaments or in payment for wars which wise and just policy would render unnecessary, then it is positively a good thing for the community that a considerable fraction should remain at the disposal of the most capable men, among whom there will at least be a proportion who will find good social use for it, and in particular many who will use it for experiment in the working out of new ideas. It is one thing to give free service to the community in accordance with one's own conception of the common interest; it is quite another to be constrained to serve the State which is the community's very imperfect organ. In a community very wisely organized with a single eye to the best human interests payment by vital costs would suffice to harmonize the producer's interest, for everything outside his industrial duties would find its suitable provision in the ideal order. But in the imperfect compromise represented by the best-known State it is otherwise. It is in the larger interest of the common good itself that private interests should maintain themselves, and that in particular capable men should be able to make their own way, provided always that they pay as they go, i.e. that their advancement is secured not by useless or injurious activities, but by sound social service.[1]

If remuneration is proportionate to value, what is the proportion to be, and how is value to be assessed? (1) If we are comparing different quantities of the same quality the case is comparatively simple. Payment by output, generally known as a piece-rate, provides for each worker remuneration directly proportional to output. The rate per piece must be on our first principle, such as will (as the Trade Board regulation puts it) suffice to yield to the ordinary worker the minimum time-rate. For our

[1] When Exchange is conceived as a purely external relation—that is, a taking place between two persons who have no common interest beyond the transaction—the justice which regulates it is called commutative justice, and in this event it is clear that its rule must be that of equal values alone. When it is conceived as the mutual benefit of two people whose interests are absolutely identified separate values disappear and all that is needed is that vital cost should be replaced. In a family, or between close friends, in the spiritual sphere or where high service is concerned, this is in fact the simple and sufficient rule. A political community might reach this ideal, by a development not of particular individuals, but of the great body of its members and the spirit of the common life. Equality of value would then be of no account. In the actual community we do not get such identification, and for reasons stated it is not desirable that we should merge the individual unless or until such merging should come of itself as a spiritual development. We have therefore something intermediate between exchange by value and co-operative maintenance of function, i.e. exchange in proportion to values as defined by a communal standard.

purposes the minimum time-rate must suffice to meet the workers' vital costs, and for us (here we are more strict than the Trade Boards) the ordinary worker must include the least skilled who is employed for industrial as against semi-philanthropic or disciplinary reasons. The minimum thus fixed, it is possible to exceed it by extra effort or skill, or both combined, and the excess remuneration is directly proportional to excess output. Thus the ordinary piece-rate system falls within our principle provided that the rate itself meets our minimum conditions. (2) As between different kinds of work there seems to be no standard of comparison except the economic equation of demand and supply of available ability. That is, if we ask what is really high-grade ability, the answer is that it is ability which (a) has a high value in use, i.e. makes a large contribution to the stock of wealth and well-being, and (b) is difficult to attain, and therefore rare. The exact measure of the value resting on these two factors together is most nearly yielded by the remuneration which does, in fact, just serve to call forth and maintain an adequate supply of the necessary ability. This is not to say that the operation of demand and supply is of itself a justification of payment by output. It is not so, for demand and supply are operative facts, not ethical principles. It is to say that, given payment by value of output as just—and this implies that output of the humblest kind carries the "civic wage"—it is demand and supply that measure differential values of outputs of varying quality. The measure may be criticized as subjective, but it is not subjective in the sense of yielding to individual caprice. It appeals to the normal disposition of ordinary men, and it is a part of our principle to harmonize such normal disposition with the good of the community. It contemplates the entire body of available ability standing before the open field of all possible forms of service, and supposes that when the possibilities of success and failure are taken into account all parts of the field are rendered equally attractive to effort. It does not contemplate increase or diminution of reward to any individual or section in accordance with their greater or less covetousness. Lastly, as our objective is the harmonization of real needs, we must take into account the diminishing returns in the shape of real satisfaction as incomes increase beyond the point necessary for the maintenance of function. Additions to a large income are not of the same value, personal or social, as the same additions to a small income. The movements of remuneration should therefore be diminishing increments tending to stability at some maximum point which can only be determined by experience of the limit of wealth commonly desirable in the interests of the possessor and the community.

With this limitation we must admit remuneration in proportion to the value of work done as a maxim of economic justice. The admission is of the first importance in the application of principles of justice to ideals of social organization. For the admission makes possible a system of free exchange—which will never take place except at equal values—and its denial involves a system of industry communally organized. It is thus the point of division between Socialism proper and the

Social Liberalism which seeks the harmony of the communal and the individual.[1]

Remunerative justice, then, consists in the supply of needs and maintenance of functions (*a*) by meeting all the vital costs of productive effort in full; (*b*) by the provision of increased remuneration for increased effort and for special ability. There would be no functionless wealth—that is to say (the case of the helpless apart), there would be no unearned incomes, and none earned by socially useless or injurious effort. Economic justice in general would thus consist in exchange of goods and

---

[1] Among other things the principle of payment in proportion to value of work—the standard being once fixed by the requisites of the civic minimum—solves the question of the fair remuneration of the sexes. If the value of a woman's work, all things considered, is the same as that of a man, she should receive the same pay. If it is more she should receive more, and if less, less. There is no harm in her receiving less if the man's wage is sufficient to maintain a family and if a woman does not normally maintain a family. Two things are postulated: (1) that the woman who has in fact to maintain and care for a family is entitled to State maintenance as of right for the performance of that function, (2) that a woman's minimum wage in no case falls below the needs of her individual maintenance. This last case will not practically occur if the woman's minimum is proportioned to the man's according to relative values, for it will be found that women's rates average about sixty per cent. of men's which (if the men's allow for a family of five) is far above the necessary personal minimum.

It may be added that in fixing rates for a competitive system any method but that of relative values is impracticable. If women's rates are fixed above the ordinary ratio of their value to that of men they will fail to get employment, and if below they will oust the men. The same thing applies to juniors and to the elderly. As a fact junior rates have to be kept up to counteract the tendency which easily manifests itself to dismiss adults and take juniors in their place.

THE PAYMENT OF SERVICE 171

services at equal values, where the cost of goods is determined by the payment for social services and the payment of services is reckoned from the unit which suffices on the average to meet the vital cost of the worker, subject to an increment depending on the extra value of the service and the rarity of the capacity to perform it. Where values are not so fixed, exchange at equal values, though just as between two individuals, does not yield a just economic system.

We have now reviewed the general principles of justice in their most important applications, and are in a position to sum up our account of the function of justice in ethics and of the relation of justice to equality. Justice is the principle of universality in ethics, and this means two things. It means, first, that wheresoever the relations of men extend every possible subject of good or ill has, as such, a claim upon the good. Since this claim is mutual, it follows that in a permanent community that alone can be a true good which can enter into a working whole harmonizing the goods of each and all. This brings us to the second meaning of our principle, which is that this harmony is a system in which the due of every element is determined on universal grounds in accordance with its relation to the system as a whole. The assignment of these grounds and the determination of their mutual relations is the special function of justice. Every person (indeed every element) within the system has his needs. Everyone not incapacitated has his functions. Justice has to harmonize the needs with one another and the functions with the needs. Considering needs, it effects harmony by the equal provision for equal needs, but subject to the bearing of such provision upon functions. Considering functions, it maintains that body of functions which best supplies general needs in the order of their importance, and the value of functions being determined by their utility for this purpose on the one side and the difficulty of securing their performance on the other, it harmonizes the requirements of each performer of function with those of the community by reward proportioned to the value of his work. Finally, for nonfunction and misfunction, justice supplies such curative and preventive treatment as reduces the unavoidable disharmony to its lowest terms.

In this account equality lies at the foundation of justice in the sense that every person and every function capable of harmony must be equally taken into account in framing the plan of harmony. All that is harmonizable must be harmonized, and in this fundamental respect none is before or after another. It follows that the good which one may legitimately claim all may claim, unless there is a grounded difference, and the only ultimate ground of difference is some requirement of the working system of harmony as a whole. On the other hand, the system will not in fact give to all the same function or the same provision. The distribution is proportionate in the sense in which that term includes qualitative as well as quantitative adjustment, and in this relation the equality of justice is a proportionate equality. Thus, in both relations justice is a form of equality, but what form is determined by its primary function as the moral universal—that which makes the good everywhere applicable and everywhere self-consistent in its operation.

NOTE

It may be said that the admission of sub-minimal payment (p. 159) destroys the principle of the minimum wage. Why not say simply "minimum living income should be universal. It is desirable that as many as possible should earn this income, but some cannot. Let them earn what they can and make up the balance. Prevent exploitation by all means, but do not pretend that all earn what not all can earn?" The reply is that the principle is not that all men and women, but all required in industry, must earn the minimum wage. This result, it is contended, is attainable by a readjustment of values consequent on the elimination of exploitation as a means of gain, together with other methods which have yet to be examined (see chap. ix, p. 204). But are the subnormal not required? If not, why are they employed? The reply is that they are on a marginal fringe, not indispensable but useful—on terms. Now the minimum principle says to the hirer in effect, "If you want a man's labour without question asked you must pay the full price. If you want it short of that price, questions will be asked. The worker comes under the guardianship of an impartial authority which must be satisfied that the defect is proportionate to the diminution of pay." Without the fixed minimum there is no basis from which to reckon the diminution—nor for that matter to assess any increment.

Briefly, if the contention is that what is desirable is not a minimum but a comprehensive adjustment of payment to value of services from highest to lowest, the reply is that the minimum as defined is the basis upon which all such adjustments are made. Without it the scale of payments might be complete and satisfactory in its proportions but destitute of any unit of absolute magnitude.

CHAPTER VIII

PROPERTY AND ECONOMIC ORGANIZATION

PUBLIC and private charity apart, the distribution of wealth that we have contemplated would depend entirely upon services rendered. The actual distribution of wealth in all established civilized systems depends primarily on property. We must therefore inquire what function property subserves, and how it is to be related to the principles of just distribution.

Property in general has sometimes been defined as the exclusive right to the use, enjoyment and control of things. Use and enjoyment, however, are not distinctive marks of property. As a member of an institution I may be given clothes to wear, food to eat, tools to use, a room to occupy, and they are "mine" for the time. For the purpose assigned I may have the full use and enjoyment of these things, and in the case of the food I consume it once for all, while the clothes I gradually wear out. But they are not my property. I cannot dispose of them, or use them for purposes other than the institution prescribes. It is the institution which controls them, and that it seems to be which makes them the property of the institution. The owner, however, may part with the control for a time, or for certain purposes. Thus, subject to certain rights of the landlord and certain covenants in my lease, I have the control of the house and premises which I occupy as tenant. But whatever control I enjoy, I hold of the owner as a delegated right. My trustee, again, has neither the use and enjoyment of the property which he holds for me, nor has he more than a limited control. His power of selling or otherwise dealing with the property may be seriously restricted; but though he is the nominal owner—is, e.g., registered as such at the Bank of England—it would seem that the real owner is rather the "dead hand" or, more generally, the legally perpetuated will of those who made the settlement. Thus, though we are still dealing with private property, we may—and often do—find that the ownership has become impersonal and more or less dispersed. We may, however, usefully think of all possible rights in a thing—e.g. every sort of use that can be made of it, and every sort of claim which might be advanced and upheld, to put it to such use—as constituting a complete corpus, which, taken together, would be the plenitude and entirety of property in that thing. Anyone recognized as enjoying this entire corpus would be the absolute owner of the thing. He could control it in every way physically possible, and this absoluteness implies that his control is exclusive. If anyone can at any point interfere with him, his right is not absolute. It is clear, further, that one or more of these rights might be withdrawn, possibly transferred by the owner to some one else, or perchance shared with him by others. In that case the property would be to this extent limited, divided, or even dissipated. What would remain property would be those rights of control which should be exclusively exercised by some assignable person or persons. Now, all property is of course limited by the universal rights of other people—i.e. I must not so use my property as to inflict injury on my neighbours. This is in strictness a limitation on that absoluteness of control which is considered above as constituting the plenitude of property. But such general restrictions would not, I think, be usually regarded as limiting the rights of property. They are rather restrictions applying to the owner personally as a citizen, e.g. it would be wrong—and I suppose illegal—to discharge my own gun on my own land in such a way as to endanger passers-by on a public highway. But this does not seem to be properly a restriction on any right of property, but rather on my personal conduct. On the other hand, an order under the Defence of the Realm Act to till my land in a particular way, or any restriction on its tillage by law or covenant, is a restriction on the property as such. All the power over the land left by the restriction I should still retain, and the corpus of control rights as dominated by the restriction would then constitute the substance of my property in the land.

Thus, a right of property is in general a recognized power of control over something. The right may be delegated,[1] or shared, and it may be limited in all sorts of ways by other rights of control, but so far as it extends

---

[1] The property is then in general attributed to the authority who delegates it as "owner," though if the recipient can deal freely with the right, e.g. sell it, he is the owner of that right, subject to whatever restrictions may be applicable to it, while the man from whom he derived the right is still thought of as owner of the "thing."

PROPERTY ORGANIZATION

it is exclusive, barring out the interference of others. What we call common property is either (1) strictly the property of an organized community, e.g. it is property of the State or a public body established by the State, such as a public park or a municipal tramcar; or (2) something wholly unappropriated, as the air was popularly though not quite accurately supposed to be before the rise of questions connected with aviation. Public property may be held for common use and enjoyment, as are the roads, but they are true property, and any attempt to monopolize them, even temporarily by causing an obstruction, may be forbidden. Property as such, then, is not the same thing as private property; but is simply control exercised by some definite authority; and the true antithesis to property is not socialistic ownership, but a quite anarchistic communism. A regulated communism, such as that apparently attempted by the Russian Soviets, does not abolish property, but only private property, placing or attempting to place the control of all production and distribution in the hands of the Government.

It will be clear that when we speak of the functions of property we must decide whether we are concerned with property in general, or with common property, or some form of corporate property, or private property, and it will be seen that the function is likely to be affected by the extent and nature of the right, or, conversely, by the restrictions which limit it, and also by the nature of the object over which it is exercised by its source, and even by its amount. It is quite possible, e.g., that one right of private property might serve a useful function, while another might be harmful; and to destroy one is not necessarily to impair another. It is impossible that private control of one kind of object may in general be a good thing, and public control of another kind of object a better thing, and the absence of all control over a third object an equally good thing. And we ought not to regard criticisms of any given kind of property as criticisms of all kinds of property.

In quite general terms, property seems to serve one function. It is a form of regulated control. What is not property at all may be used or misused by anyone; and if it is limited in amount and desirable in kind its use may breed disputes. If it is the assigned property of some one, there is no disputing about its use, for there is a definite authority assigned for its control. In a world composed exclusively of right-minded people there might be no need of property, private or collective. As things are, anarchistic communism can be safely applied only to the unlimited and unspoilable. Things owned by the State can be held open to common use and enjoyment if they are not easily injured and cannot be monopolized. Roads, parks, public places, a drinking-fountain can be so used subject only to very general regulations as to good behaviour. There is a working communism of use and enjoyment in such cases which has been found appropriate under suitable conditions, and which is quite different from the use of public property on payment, e.g., of a municipal tramcar on payment of the fare. The point that concerns us for the moment is that common use and enjoyment are possible only of things which cannot be misused, or of which the misuse is easily prevented, and that they may still be subject to the ultimate control of public (or, for that matter, of private) ownership. The first and most general function of property, then, is to give control of things to an assigned authority, and such assignment appears in general necessary to prevent disputes and misuse. This control carries with it a measure of liberty and a definite form of responsibility. The liberty is naturally realized most clearly in the case of private property. It is true that, subject to whatever be the moral or legal limitations of ownership, "I can do what I like with my own." This distinguishes it from that which is not my own, but is assigned to me for a purpose. My own clothes I can wear as I please, wear them out if I please, cut them up and make them into different garments, sell, destroy, or give them away. An institution might provide me with equally good clothing, but if it retained property therein would not give me the same freedom. So far as the direction of my life and the exercise of my faculties depend on the free disposal (as distinguished from the prescribed use) of material things, it depends on my possession of property. What is true of the individual is also true of a corporation or the community. If the State borrows money for a particular purpose, it is bound in its use of the money—bound morally, even if there be no remedy against misapplication. What is its own, e.g. its ships, it can deal with as it will—break them up if it chooses or dispose of them to private people or another Government. In respect to its own property it is, like the individual, free. The essential difference, then, between property in a thing and the defined use of a thing is freedom of choice as between all the purposes to which the thing may be put. Thus, in general, the right of property is a branch of freedom, and this holds of property in general, though obviously of importance mainly in relation to private property.

This freedom does away with certain obvious responsibilities, but it imposes on the owner a kind of natural or physical responsibility. If he is independent of others he is the more dependent on the physical characteristics of his possession. If he wastes or spoils it, he has no one to fall back upon to replace it. He cannot both eat his cake and have it; whereas, if he is dependent on some one else, that person, finding him hungry, must decide—perhaps arbitrarily—whether he is to have another meal or go without. Property, then, along with freedom, confers the particular kind of responsibility involved in self-dependence. This, again, has its most obvious bearing in relation to individuals, but is in reality quite as important for States, the more so as many people seem to be invariably persuaded that in this relation the maxim of the cake does not apply, but that States can expend their resources without diminishing or needing to repair them. To appreciate the price that they pay for their desires is no less necessary for communities than for private persons.

If property is the economic basis of freedom and self-dependence, the possession of *some* property is desirable for individuals, and for any corporate body that has to direct its own affairs. What sort of property, and under what conditions, we have not yet asked. We reach this question, however, as soon as we observe that the property which confers freedom on the owner may, at the same time, limit or destroy the freedom of another. For example, a man may have direct property in another, e.g. in a slave or, by a law now recognized as semi-obsolete, in his wife. Here we have one of the cases in which the freedom of one is the unfreedom of another. And this is still true if it is the State who owns the slave. Hence, avowed property in persons has in general been discarded, and we should find most people agree that property is a right over things, while slavery illegitimately treats persons as things. The definition, however, has its difficulties when we seek a general application. Copyright or patent right is not so much a power over material things which can always be assigned, but rather a power of restraining others from publishing a book or making an implement. Essentially, therefore, it is a power over persons, and as such needs to be very carefully watched.

But, looking a little further, we find many forms of property which involve power over other persons. I do not here speak of the restriction which exclusive ownership obviously involves in the use of the thing owned by anyone but the owner without his permission. I speak of restriction of liberty in other respects. The owner of an intervening strip of land, by restricting the right of way, may, of course, debar his neighbours on either side from the full use of their lands, and this is a consequence which law and custom are compelled to take into consideration. But, further than this, the owner of land may be in a position to determine the means by which many people can earn their living. In a small way this is true of every one with a shilling to spend. He may give his custom to Mrs. Jones or Mrs. Brown as he will, and to that extent affects their prosperity. The extent of this power varies partly with the nature of the property, partly with the distribution of ownership. If the property is important and limited, ownership may involve a partial or complete monopoly, carrying with it a considerable, perhaps a fundamental, power over the lives of many, and this will hold true whether the ownership be in private or public hands. As soon as all the coal, or even the bulk of the coal, or even the bulk of the steam coal, is in one hand, be it in the hand of the State or of the Miners' Federation, or of a trust, that hand controls the industry that depends on coal. If, again, there is no monopoly, but wealth is very unevenly distributed, then the possessors of capital have advantages in contracting with workers which give them a very large measure of control over labour. Thus, if property is in one aspect freedom, it is under another aspect power; and which aspect is the more important depends on the nature of the property and its distribution.

In economics, as in other spheres, freedom is a double-edged term. It is comparatively easy to compass freedom in certain respects. The difficulty is to avoid losing it in that very act in some other respect. The unfreedom which has been most keenly felt in modern industry rests on the dependence of the worker without capital on the owner of the means of production. Now, the peasant proprietor who tills his own fields with his own cattle and his own plough is free from this sort of dependence (provided that he avoids debt). But he is not free from the land. He cannot, like the landless labourer, betake himself anywhere where he can sell his labour to the best advantage, but is tied to a certain avocation which he can abandon only to launch out into much the same uncertainty and insecurity by which the proletarian is beset. The workman, again, who seeks freedom in combination may put himself on an equality with his employer, or may perchance dispense with him; but, of course, enters into the restraints of associated life. Different schools have seen economic freedom (broadly speaking) in one or other of these directions, but have not, perhaps, always realized the compensating losses in either case. On one point, however, both parties would agree—that he who is wholly dependent on another for the opportunity of maintaining himself is also virtually devoid of freedom, of the means of guiding his own life and working out his own purposes in his own way.

Meanwhile, what we have learnt is that in economics property is on the one side freedom, on the other power. Now, there seem to be two ways of working towards general economic freedom and reconciling it with power. The first is by the method of individualist production—the peasant-proprietor, the one-man business. This method is the economic expression of that view of liberty which regards it as an emancipation of individual life from the social nexus. Accordingly, even if sound in principle, it would only have a minor and diminishing place in a highly industrialized society. The alternative method is the economic expression of liberty as a social function and as dependent on social control. On this method property as economic power must be vested in the last resort in a self-governing community, while the individual will require property—as distinct from the prescribed use and permitted enjoyment of material things—for the free conduct of his personal life. Economic power will be based on and exercised for the promotion of liberty if (1) it is so organized that any individual can, according to his capacity, have an effective voice in collective decisions, and (2) if the industrial government secures to every capable individual the right to work, to choose and vary his occupation so far as the requirements of industrial organization permit, to obtain advancement by merit, to exercise personal initiative within the limits defined by the accepted system of rights, and to enjoy the reward of service as his out-and-out personal property. Further, the worker should be able, without being reduced to dependence on any outside authority, to provide against the ordinary contingencies of life, sickness, accident, old age and unavoidable employment, and to maintain his children till they are able to work for themselves.[1] For all these purposes he

[1] A difficulty arises here which has both a theoretical and practical interest. The claim to maintenance, e.g. in sickness and old age, may be based on needs and is then irrespective of earnings. In fact, the helpless have, as we have always insisted, such a claim, and that as a matter of justice and right. At the same time we contended above that it is not a claim to property but to provision for a specific object. It is a lien which every member of the community has as a member of the community on the common resources, but not a title to so much money to be at that member's free disposal. Now it may be asked, In which category does the maintenance of the worker in sickness, unemployment, and old age really fall? He has earned this maintenance, we agree. But he would

requires the free disposal of adequate material means—that is, he requires an adequate income which is his out-and-out property, by which, moreover, he can build up a home and surround himself with those little personal belongings which constitute property on its most human side. This is the measure of the individual's claim to property, and it coincides precisely with the requirements of economic justice on his behalf as set out in the last

also have a right to it as a human being. Does it matter in which way we regard it? The reply is that if we regard it as earned we shall hold it the worker's business to provide for it. It will be the business of the social economy to secure him pay sufficient to cover all risks, and it will be his part to make the necessary insurances. At the same time the standard of maintenance which he will expect will be one corresponding not to his prime needs. but to his ordinary earnings, which will not be less but may be materially higher. But here arises the difficulty that whatever his earnings a man may in fact fail to make the necessary provision. Then even though it is his own fault we cannot let him go short of his prime needs. Hence on this method we may in certain cases be called upon as it were to pay twice over. The community then seems to have a right—correlative to its duty of meeting prime needs—to call on the capable individual to provide for such needs. This principle underlies compulsory insurance in respect of the bare minima necessary for prime needs, and would, I think, justify it if rates of wages were uniformly high enough to be conceived as covering such risks. But in view of the extreme difficulty—inherent, as will be seen later, in the economic organization—of securing such rates universally, there is a great deal to be said for the view that the community should bear the full cost of insurance to meet prime needs, giving facilities to the individual to add thereto at his pleasure. This, however, must be taken as the fulfilment of a debt by the community to the worker and not as derogatory in any way from his right to enjoy such maintenace as something he has earned. The problem, however, differs according to the nature of the risk, and may be discussed later in connection with the general organization of industry.

chapter, merely emphasizing freedom in the direction of personal life as an element in his due. On the other hand, for the sake of liberty, the final directing power in industry must be in communal hands, since, if exercised by individuals, it gives them the disposal of the lives of others. What form this power is to take, by what representative organs it can be exercised, whether it involves direct management or an ultimate and reserved control, are most difficult questions which arise as soon as any attempt is made to translate principle into practice. For the present we must be content to affirm that property, so far as it implies the ultimate control of the industrial mechanism, is a communal function, whereas the right of the individual is that of effective participation in common decisions and of the most direct participation in those which most nearly concern him.

What property would be necessary to the community for this purpose, and in particular from what sources would it be derived? We are clearly contemplating a certain apportionment between the individual and the community. Would the apportionment based on the claims of freedom coincide with that based on economic justice? So far as the individual's share is concerned, we have seen reason to think that it would. We might infer that any surplus remaining would fall to the community, and it would remain to ask whether the enjoyment of this surplus would assure to the community the necessary control. But it will be well to check and supplement our account of economic justice by considering the matter afresh from the communal point of view. If our account is correct, the claims of the community and the individual ought to cover the whole field, and ought to satisfy the claims of economic justice and liberty. To test this we must consider the various elements in wealth, and the precise ground of their apportionment as between the community and the individual.

CHAPTER IX

SOCIAL AND PERSONAL FACTORS IN WEALTH

THERE are broadly two grounds on which the claims of the community on available wealth may be based. (1) The community, like the individual, performs certain functions which require their due return, apart from which the would be starved, just as the individual's functions may be starved. These functions are in part conscious and deliberate. The State organization is to begin with the basis of security, and therewith (among other things) of property itself. That consideration alone gives to the community the last word in declaring what rights of property it will recognize, and on what terms. Ordinary thought is far too apt to conceive property as absolutely inherent in the individual and all taxation as a process of depriving him—it may be with due cause, but still depriving him—of something which is unquestionably his own. This view is as one-sided as that which gives to the State absolute right of disposal without regard to any ethical considerations. But not only is the State organization the basis of property, it may also be used to increase and improve property, for example, by measures in the interests of social progress. These do not necessarily bring any money return to the State coffers. For instance, public education produces a population far more capable of earning wealth, but the wealth so earned is not paid over directly to the State. Similarly, a drainage system is good for the public health, but those who enjoy the result do not pay by results. In such cases—and all improvements of governmental organization may be brought under the same head—services are given by the community without direct payment in return. The actual cost of the services has to be met by the general taxation, and there is no doubt this indirect return, that from a more prosperous community the same tax will bring in a larger revenue. But there is no direct return from each individual proportioned to the services rendered to the individual. Yet clearly, there is a great increment in the value of life diffused among members of society which ought to feed and sustain the organized efforts that produce it.

But this is not all. Partly as a result of the organized efforts of society, but more largely through the mere fact of social life, and the tacit co-operation of many minds, society on the whole grows, the arts of life improve, population thickens. There is a total increment of wealth. What we take at first blush for the contribution of an individual to this growth is not his contribution alone. He absorbs from his society, he comes into a capital of organized knowledge and skill; he adds something to it but does not create it. The most individual production is largely a social production. Again, much of a man's work may lie in organizing others, and what these others are, what skilled and trustworthy workmen, for instance, he finds to his hand, is determined by large social causes. Thus, individual production is penetrated through and through by the social factor, and here again, we can see that if the social factor does not get its due return, disorganization ensues. For example: as the industry of a town expands, so does the population, and as population grows so does the value of the land. The people must have houses to live in, and their mere numbers force up rents. Now this added land value is not any one man's creation. It is a social product. The ground landlord, in particular, need never have done a hand's turn in the process of making the town; but his ownership has enabled him to skim off all the cream of value, which is due to a complex congeries of social factors. If this value came back to the town collectively the increase of population would pay its way. The town would have the funds for building, planning, beautifying itself. Because English towns have been starved of their natural sources of revenue they are ugly, crowded and mean. Population is stimulated to growth without provision for the due nourishment of growth, and just as there is disorganization when the individual is made to function without due maintenance so there is disorganization when society attempts to function without due maintenance.

The performance of functions, conscious or unconscious, is thus one of the grounds on which the community has a claim to the wealth produced by its members. There is another quite distinct ground at which we must now glance.

Neither individual nor social productivity is directly responsible for all the wealth that exists. There is wealth attributable to the efforts of no living individual,

SOCIAL FACTORS IN WEALTH

nor to the social organization. Such, for example, are the natural resources of the soil. There is, again, inherited wealth, produced directly by the efforts of dead people, and secured to the living owner by society. Social factors may have contributed to the production of such wealth, but we cannot call it as a whole a social product. But neither is it the product of the present owner. To whom, then, should it on our principles belong?

Since property confers exclusive rights there must, to justify individual ownership, be some reason for giving to some definite individual rights as against others. If there is no such special reason the basis of exclusive ownership fails, and all have an equal right to participate, i.e. the only rational claim is that of the community. Now, the only claims that we have recognized are the existence of a need or the performance of a function. These yield a general claim on the resources of society, but none on unearned wealth as such. There is, therefore, no direct economic necessity for recognizing private property in natural resources or in inherited wealth, and these are in fact the main sources of functionless wealth, economic inequality, and the preponderant power of certain classes over others. The ground on which they are defended is that though the individual owner performed or need perform no function in order to acquire this kind of wealth, yet in general, economic functions are better fulfilled by private than by public ownership. Thus, new countries have parcelled out their land to individuals to secure population and economic development. We must admit that it is better that the function of development should be fulfilled by this method than not to be fulfilled at all. Private property here performs a function in default of its fulfillment by a properly constituted organ of the community. None the less, the community is letting go something which is legitimately its own when it allows natural resources to fall as exclusive property into private hands.

Inheritance and bequest, again, have their use as long as the community does not make adequate provision for the youth and helplessness of all its members. As permanent institutions they are defended as a stimulus to production and accumulation.

The first of these functions is, however, performed by the remuneration of the producer in accordance with the value of his product, which was, in fact, justified on this ground among others. It is the second function on which defenders of the "capitalist system" now principally rely. It is pointed out that the bulk of the yearly savings of the nation come out of the large surplus incomes of rich individuals and are induced largely by the desire to perpetuate the family wealth and position, and it is feared that if this source of saving were cut off accumulation would cease. This is to assume that the community lacks either the means or the sense to save. If the community were the principal owner of land and capital it would have regular sources of revenue— the main sources from which the large incomes of the present are derived. It would have to balance the needs of the present and the future, just as any private firm has to do, and on the whole it would be in a position to take a longer view. The necessity of developments

SOCIAL FACTORS IN WEALTH 193

involving the sinking of capital would be constantly pressed upon it, and the question whether it would deal with them wisely and well is a part of the general question of good government—a question which I freely admit underlies any proposal for the extension of communal functions, but not this one any more than the others. It must be added that if it is a question of sound economy, there could hardly be a more wasteful method of securing accumulation than the present, particularly as interpreted in the argument in question. For this argument assumes incomes so large that saving becomes a matter of little or no sacrifice—an item of uncertain magnitude salved from a waste of luxury expenditure. A socialist may be pardoned if he thinks it worth trying to get the saving without the waste.

There is a much more human argument for inheritance in the shape of bequest which cannot, I think, be entirely ignored. Parents cannot brook the thought that any child may for want of effort on their part be forced to live on a standard to which it has not been brought up. A very deep and valuable human impulse is thwarted if permanent provision for children is rendered impossible. Now the main duty in this relation that parents owe their children is education, and there can be no reasonable objection to full provision for this need by bequest. On the other hand children ought to be brought up to provide for themselves, and to live on inheritance is to enjoy functionless wealth. Yet, to take a single example, it would be exceedingly cruel to deprive a parent of the right to make provision out of his own earnings for a delicate child beyond the somewhat bare maintenance which is all that can be reasonably expected from the common funds, and a father or mother may be aware of particular needs in a child which no public system is likely to recognize. Even if we look on the matter more severely as one of principle there is something to be said on the parent's side, for we have contended that his earnings are his out and out property. He can certainly accumulate them for his lifetime, and it follows that he can give them away. It does not follow that he should have the right of bequest which makes it easy for him to enjoy the income of his accumulation for life and also the comfort of providing for his child after death. The solution which suggests itself is that if he wishes to endow the child he should do so in his lifetime by gift instead of at death by bequest. This is in effect to limit such provision to cases in which and to amounts of which the need is strongly felt. It also prevents the formation of permanent unearned family wealth, for though the child in turn could make similar provision he could only do so (apart from earnings of his own) at the expense of his own share, so that the amount passed on successively diminishes. It recognizes the solidarity of parent and child by allowing the child to live—permanently it may be—on wealth earned by its father, without permitting the apparently inevitable consequence of the perpetuity of family property. Paradoxical as this seems to be, it is both practicable in operation and true to a real and deep distinction of feeling—for parental feeling is one thing and the desire to found and perpetuate a family another, and one with more pride in it, than love.

Subject to this understanding, then, we are free to maintain that personally accumulated capital is personal property, and that hereditary capital should be communal property, i.e. that property in general should pass to the community at death.[1] Neither natural resources nor the wealth of past generations would in general be regarded as proper objects of private ownership in a community which is fulfilling adequately the functions of a common life.

So far we have distinguished personal and public sources of wealth, together with no-man's wealth, to which we think the community has the true claim. We must now distinguish social and unsocial elements in wealth.

The distinction between production which is socially desirable and the reverse, is of minor interest in pure economics, but is fundamental to an ethical treatment of industry and property. Within the mass of what we call wealth, is to be found the material basis of the Common Good—the sum, that is, of those objects which are necessary for the healthy development of individuals, and for the promotion of the common life. Except in an ideal society, what is called wealth is by far the wider conception of the two, for it includes everything that satisfies human desires, and everything therefore which, if it can be appropriated, can also be exchanged at a

[1] It need hardly be said that this does not apply to "personalia," such as furniture, books, etc., for which exemptions can easily be made.

price.[1] If we could imagine the production of wealth determined more and more by the actual requirements of the Common Good, this difference would tend to disappear. Either the effective desires of men would come to approximate to the standard of the desirable, or at any rate those which diverged would have no means of satisfaction. Till this consummation is reached, actual wealth, and what may be called for the moment social wealth, are different things, much of actual wealth being from the social point of view "illth." An insanitary house, for example, may be a source of wealth to its owner. It will be rated at such and such a figure, and if we compute the rateable value of the town in which it stands, or the national income returnable under "Schedule A," it will figure as an item in the addition. Yet socially considered, it should probably be treated as a minus quantity in the enumeration of the conditions of a healthy life. Other items of "wealth" are more difficult to value socially. Their worth may depend on the use to which they are put, or on the proportions in which they are distributed. Of the national expenditure on alcohol, for example, one might say that there is a maximum point up to which it is socially valuable, and beyond which it becomes useless and in rapidly accelerating degree harmful. Opinions would differ a good deal about the position of this maximum point. Some would

[1] As personal qualities, skill and intellect are so exchangeable they also rank ordinarily as wealth. They are not, however, parts of the material basis of the Common Good, but rather so far as they are good qualities, parts of the Common Good itself. This, then, is another point of differentiation between the two aggregates mentioned.

place it as nearly as possible at zero. Others would raise it sufficiently to allow for "moderate" drinking, but very few, I imagine, would deny that the maximum point is handsomely passed by the production and consumption of alcoholic liquors in this country. If that is so, all the millions spent on this article beyond the maximum figure as wealth in statistics of the national income, but would figure as minus quantities in those ideal statistics that we are imagining.[1]

For the present, the point which concerns us is, that the production and distribution and consumption of wealth and everything that has to do therewith, is conditioned, ethically speaking, by the function of wealth as the material basis of personal and social life. All rights, all obligations affecting industrial and commercial life, rest for their ultimate moral obligation on this func-

[1] The distinction between "trade net product" and "social net product" is carefully drawn by Professor Pigou, who discusses (*Economics of Welfare,* Pt. II, chap. v) possible cases of divergence. Thus of the liquor trade he writes, "To enable the social net product to be inferred from the trade net product of a sovereign invested in this form of production, the industry should, as Mr. Bernard Shaw observes, be debited with the extra costs in policemen and prisons which it indirectly makes necessary." Professor Pigou's social net product, however, is the contribution of an industry to the National Dividend, and as the measure of the National Dividend he finds himself obliged (Pt. I, chap. iii) to accept on the whole a money standard owing to the impossibility of any estimate of unpaid services. To meet the paradoxes resulting from this use of terms he reserves the right to use the term in a wider sense where to do so will help discussion. It is clear that all mutual service, whether paid or not, enters into the true national wealth. It is clear also (to take one of Professor Pigou's illustrations) that the defilement of natural beauty is a loss to the nation to be set against the development of a coal field, though

tion of industry and commerce. The actual production and distribution of wealth are to be criticized from this point of view, and are, so far as possible, to be guided thereby, so that what is produced may be not only "wealth," but "social wealth." This conception of control, however, is to be taken with all the limitations and explanations given in discussing liberty. Production for personal satisfaction is socially justified, so far as that satisfaction contributes to the development of personality, while inflicting no loss on others, and the conception of individuality as an element in well-being has its place in the sphere of industry. This being understood, we may lay down that not merely the work of any individual, but the value of an industrial system is to be judged on the side of production, not by the total wealth it produces

---

it is a loss which cannot ordinarily be measured in money. The "social wealth" of the text would clearly differ from the National Dividend in taking equal account of services, whether paid or unpaid, and further in differentiating between the sum of satisfied desires and the sum of reasonable and healthy desires which obtain satisfaction. This sum appears so remote from any possibility of statistical measure that it may seem useless to speak of it. But this is not altogether so. In particular cases we may be confident that something which is producing income is doing social harm, e.g. a demoralizing publication. Probably such social harm will ultimately have an economic reaction, and so might be reflected in the National Dividend. If that happened regularly and speedily the National Dividend would be a fair rough measure of social wealth, but it is likely that a good deal of the effect takes a long time to work itself out and is but partially reflected in the economic system. I can hardly suppose that the destruction of natural beauty has of itself an economic effect even over a long period at all comparable to the loss that it inflicts in things never measurable in money.

SOCIAL FACTORS IN WEALTH 199

as measurable in money, nor by any material standard, but by its ethical value as serving the needs of the community and the development of the social personality.

Not only are there a social and unsocial wealth, but there are social and unsocial methods of making wealth. Thus, the individual may enrich himself without adding any corresponding increment of wealth to society. A man may buy cheap and hold stock till it becomes dear. The process may or may not be useful to society. It is useful in an unregulated industry in so far as it tends to stimulate production when it is deficient, and to check it when superabundant. The profits made by those who thus intelligently forecast the market may be regarded as of the nature of a payment for the regulation of industry. They may with equal justice be regarded as a tax which keen-sighted individuals can put upon society on account of its deficiencies in organization. The mere speculator who enters into the business of buying and selling with a view to the chances of the market seems to fulfil no function, but only to aggravate fluctuations of prices which makes the reward of the producers the more uncertain. It would seem (*a*) to be a legitimate object of society to render this source of individual profit unavailable by assisting as far as possible the work of organization, and (*b*) in the meanwhile to reduce the profits of mere speculation as far as possible by taxation, thereby enhancing the degree of socially-useful foresight necessary to make the working of the financial middleman a paying business.

(2) In all exchange the greater advantage goes to the stronger purchaser. He may be stronger through his

existing economic position, or through special skill in bargaining. Neither of these adds to social wealth. The qualities which make a good bargainer are rather anti-social, and the good bargain achieved by superiority of economic position does not represent any proportionate increment in the social value of the product sold. Profit on price, then, so far as due to such causes, is not a reward of social service. As accruing to the individual it represents a tax on others.

(3) The same considerations apply to all profits accruing from the possession of differential advantages in production, except so far as they depend on and correspond to differences of personal ability in organizing and executing production. The price of an article being fixed by demand and supply, the owner of any differential advantages enabling him to produce it at lower cost, is able to secure to himself the balance as profit. This again is of the nature of a tax levied by the individual on industry.

We arrive at the conclusion that profit on price, except so far as it results from socially serviceable qualities such as able organization, is wealth to the individual which makes no net addition to the wealth of the whole community. It is therefore of the nature of a tax levied on the community by individuals. Good social organization would abolish that tax, and, failing that possibility, would endeavour to cancel as much of it as possible by social taxation.

Reviewing the several constituents of wealth we find that the community would be the owner of land and all natural resources and of all capital accumulated by past generations. The individual would have as his own property his salary and personal accumulations. This partition, while conserving for the individual what we previously assigned to him, gives to the community, as we anticipated, the entire surplus and therewith the ultimate control of industry through the ownership of land and accumulated capital. The point left undecided is the element of profit, and with it the question of the immediate direction of industry. Profits are the essential element in private production. The competitive producer takes the risk, enjoys the profit, or bears the loss, and on the whole looks to the result for his "wages of management." Now, if we suppose that the community has (1) secured the fair treatment of all employees; (2) eliminated the possibilities of making gain by anti-social methods; (3) taken to itself the rents and interest on inherited capital, then the residue is value created by social service. There seems, then, to be no economic injustice in leaving it to the individual. But at this point very large questions of organization arise. To leave an element of profit to the producer means in substance to maintain the immediate direction of industry by private enterprise. Undoubtedly under the conditions laid down this direction would be under public control. But on the one side it may be asked whether such control would be sufficient to secure the liberty of employees and the interest of consumers. On the other hand, it may be asked whether an efficient form of communal organization can be devised to supersede private enterprise, and in particular whether State-managed industry is the only alternative or whether there may not be forms of management which secure liberty, just partition of product and efficiency better than either State management or private enterprise. It may also be asked whether there are not other ethical considerations bearing on profit which we have not yet taken into account. In fact, we stand here at the border line between State Socialism proper and the semi-Socialism or Social Liberalism to which most modern communities seem to be committed, between public management and public control. It will be necessary to examine the question further with a view to the ethical problem involved and to the various forms of organization which have been suggested. It is of high importance to remark here that while we cannot have private enterprise without profit and loss borne by the owner, we can and must have profit or loss in any industry or branch of industry, however organized. Strictly this holds true even if there is no exchange at all, but the point is most easily seen if we suppose a price at which commodities are sold or merely charged to the account of private individuals under a State-organized system of production. If a State department is to pay its way the price must cover the expense of producing the goods. Now, the expense of producing the goods is not constant. Some part will be produced more cheaply than others. If the price covers the average cost then there will be loss on all the goods that cost more, and profit on all the goods that cost less than the average. It will be seen that in substance this would hold, even if the goods were not priced but distributed equally for a return of labour service. In a competitive system economists show that the price will be near to the amount which will cover the most expensive goods. Hence there is profit on all the rest (though a good deal of this profit may be absorbed in payments of the nature of rent which are made for standing advantages in production owned and let out by private individuals). In any case, there is a wide stretch between the cost of the marginal goods—those which barely pay their way—and the most profitable goods. If we abolish private enterprise entirely it would be possible by fixing prices at such a point as would fully meet the needs of all producers to secure the entire surplus available for common purposes. If on the other hand we admit private enterprise, we cannot fix prices, nor do we obtain the whole surplus. That is where as a community we lose, and private enterprise has to prove that it can make up for the loss by superior organization.

But there is this further point. If we can fix prices in any industry where we will, it may be (1) convenient to fix them at the marginal point, i.e. high enough to secure that the most expensive goods pay their way. The community then enjoys the whole surplus collectively, but users of the particular commodity have to pay highly. Hence, alternatively, it may be (2) convenient to fix the price lower, in which case we shall lose on the more expensive goods and our collective surplus will be reduced. This latter is the pooling arrangement suggested for the adjustment of the price of coal to the needs of consumers on the one side and the cost of labour on the other. If the price of coal is to suffice to cover the costs of the poorest mine in the Forest of Dean it is going to allow a very large profit to the richest colliery in the Rhondda valley. This is very bad economy if the profit is all destined to pass into private hands, but not if it is to enrich the community. If the coal mines were communally owned, the argument for reducing prices below the level required by the poorest mine kept working might be that coal is so necessary that the poorest householder or most struggling industrial concern ought not to have difficulty in securing it. This is an argument which can be urged with varying degrees of force in a number of necessary services. It should be clearly recognized that it proposes in effect the endowment of certain classes of goods or services, whereby those who make special use of those goods or services profit at the expense of others. We cannot here enter into the detailed discussion of the circumstances under which such endowment may be justifiable, but from the nature of the case it would only seem to apply in exceptional circumstances.

The alternative method of meeting certain needs of all wage-earners and all citizens alike out of surplus has more to recommend it. If any element in the cost of living is provided universally and gratuitously the wage necessary to cover the "civic minimum" is by so much reduced, and the cost of production falls accordingly. Some part of wages, then, is taken out of surplus, or rather replaced by a public endowment derived from surplus. The reasons for resorting to this method of payment are (1) that owing to the wide gap between the most and the least profitable production the proportion of wealth taken up by "surplus" is large, and it is difficult to secure the requisite remuneration of all producers so as to cover all needs in the case of the least efficient workers, who are apt to congregate in the least efficient works.

(2) There are particular needs which ought on no account to be stinted, e.g. education, sanitation, etc.—needs which ought to be supplied to the individual, not only for his sake, but for that of the community. There seems no strong reason against supplying such needs universally at the expense of the communal surplus, provided (1) that the funds are available, and (2) that the main responsibility for supporting his own household, and therefore along with his wife directing its economy and the joint life, remain fully secured to the individual. Subject to this condition, to which on the whole trend of our interpretation of property the highest importance must attach, the provision of common needs gratuitously or below cost price may often be good economy and is a useful method of extending the "civic minimum" to all classes without unduly raising "marginal costs."[1]

[1] The augmentation of wages and the provision of needs are complementary methods of securing the civic minimum of income for all members of the community. The first method is intrinsically desirable for the sake of liberty and responsibility, the second is intrinsically desirable in the case of special needs. Apart from such cases one would rather see minimum wages raised than State provision increased. But as a practical method of obtaining the end it may prove feasible to bring a larger percentage of all workers within the circle of those willingly employed if by extra provision of needs cash wages may be lowered. It must, however, be acknowledged that as the provision increases the border between eleemosynary provision and genuine earning by fair *quid pro quo* of work becomes an uncertain and wavering line.

CHAPTER X

INDUSTRIAL ORGANIZATION

ETHICALLY, two main arguments may be advanced against production for private profit under social control. The first is that the reward thus secured to the function of management is irregular and unequal. The element of fortune cannot be eliminated, and when the best is done it will remain the case that some will come off badly and others too well. To this it may be replied (1) that in compensation for risk there is the joy of ownership, the great gift of freedom within social limits of developing an industry in one's own way, striking out new lines and enjoying initiative. If this is a compensation to the producer, it is also, when all illegitimate means of profit-making are stopped, a gain to society which profits by good experiments when it has learnt how to arrest bad ones. It may be added (2) that as there is a type of character which prefers certainty and routine, so there is a type which prefers risk and adventure, and both types—the latter within the bounds which we assume to be laid down—are of value in their place. Excessive profits might be curbed by taxation, and in any case accumulation by inheritance—the main source of grave inequalities—is taken as barred. On this count, therefore, though profit is not so regular and nicely adjusted

INDUSTRIAL ORGANIZATION 207

a reward of management as is a fixed salary, it may be maintained that it is a more appropriate reward of fluctuating, unmeasurable services like enterprise and initiative, and the result is to suggest that private undertakings are of social value in proportion as these qualities are desirable in a given sphere of industry.

The second argument against private profit is that it is a low motive. A man should be content with that which is enough to sustain him in his function, concentrate his energies on its performance, and leave the rest to the community. To this it may be replied (a) that though social service is the higher motive not all men will feel in this way, and society may get the best out of certain types by giving them the opportunities that they seek. Further than this, (b) with the chance of profit a man takes the risks of failure. He assumes a responsibility which the salaried man avoids, and he may assume it precisely for the sake of freedom to carry out his own ideas and see how they will work out. Finally, (3) if profit is a poor motive the necessity of avoiding loss is at least a valuable economic safeguard, and one that is not always realized with sufficient force where loss and gain are diffused through a community. Private enterprise has this merit, that accounts must at least balance, or it rapidly becomes impossible to carry on. It is far more difficult to drive home the same necessity in communal transactions where losses are disguised in the shape of rising prices and increased discomfort, but there is no actual stoppage of production by the impossibility of obtaining further credit. No doubt at long last the community which is spending more than it earns must arrive at bankruptcy, but the disaster is so much the greater because there is no one behind the community, as the community is behind the individual, to save it from absolute destruction when bankruptcy arrives.

We conclude that on ethical grounds there are certain advantages in the private conduct of industry, assuming that all the conditions laid down above have been fulfilled. These advantages are proportionate to the value of personal initiative and enterprise in the industry, and are overbalanced by the obvious ethical advantages of social responsibility for industry where stabilized methods, regularity and routine are the predominant features. In other words, there is no such radical superiority of one method over the other as would debar us from asking which method in general or in a particular case will prove itself most efficient, and in fact afford to the community the greatest net yield. To gain any light on this question we must ask what methods of social management are available to replace private management. Three such types have been propounded:

(1) The most obvious method of social management is that of the State or the Municipality. Municipal management of public services has on the whole been a success, and there is no reason why it should not be extended to any routine service in a suitable area, e.g. the distribution (possibly the production) of milk, of coals, of bread and other things in general demand. Municipal management, however, is of limited application because it is suited only to services possessing a definite unity for a definite area. Production and transport on the national scale would by analogy fall to State management, which in this country

has not been regarded as successful or promising. In particular, the experience of State organization in the war has not encouraged people to go further with it. In large part these failures or partial failures are due to the traditions of a Civil Service which has grown up rather to check and control things than to move and initiate. But there is also a great difficulty in securing any effective popular control of a State organization, and a national bureaucracy, however emphatically the principle may be stated that it is the servant of the people, is in fact strong enough and remote enough from the mass of the population to make itself in practice their master. The interest of a bureaucracy is to avoid trouble. It therefore dislikes initiative, clings to safety, and prefers form to substance. It must have a good paper answer to complaints and then it can go home easy in mind. Men of this temper are selected as "safe" for promotion, while too much ability in a subordinate position is dangerous. Hence the marked peculiarity of the Civil Service that when a man becomes really master of a job, that is the time to turn him out of it. We can imagine many of these peculiarities eradicated by patient and persistent criticism. Just as we have with difficulty evolved an honest Civil Service, so we might evolve an enterprising Civil Service, and a popularly-controlled Civil Service. But the goal appears so remote that people anxious for social control have looked in other directions.

(2) According to one school, the whole theory of the State as the organ of industry is mistaken. The State is the organ of the consumer, and industry should not be

organized by the consumer but by the producer. The producer is the man who knows his job. He is far more intimately and directly interested in the details of production than the consumer, and he can be organized into a Guild with his fellows, which Guild will exercise a real and effective democratic control, because all its members will know what they are about and will have a living interest in the common decisions. Industrial self-government means the government of production by the organized body of producers. If it is urged that the Guild would then become a monopolistic body which might exploit the public, the reply is that there must be a Congress of Guilds, which should even include a body specially representative of consumers as such, to lay down the general conditions of exchange. The internal affairs of each industry would then be determined by the Guild for that industry, within which, moreover, there are to be constituent guilds and committees organizing the various sectional interests, but subject to certain conditions which would be agreed by all the sections into which the community would be organized. But though this is a tempered monopoly, it still is monopoly. The Guild is to have all the strings of an industry in its hands. Apparently it will have absolute power to decide whether the industry is to be expanded or contracted, whether new processes are to be introduced or not; I do not see how it could be denied the power of deciding whether a new member is to be admitted or not. The right to work is clearly in its hands. No doubt many abuses might be prevented by the general Congress, just as abuses in private industry can be

INDUSTRIAL ORGANIZATION 211

prevented by Parliament. But the Guild would have a recognized and admitted power which now can only be gained irregularly here and there by a particularly extensive and successful Trust. The actual power exercised by different Guilds would vary considerably. The coal miners, if they could exclude the competition of oil, would be of paramount importance because of the drastic and immediate result of any refusal on their part to produce. Railwaymen and transport workers would have a similar position, and could snap their fingers at textile operatives, engineers and agriculturists who may be producing necessaries but not necessaries of day-to-day urgency. This irregularity is, in fact, a serious element in the social situation in which we actually find ourselves, but it would be crystallized and consecrated by the Guild system.

(3) Industrial organization by the consumer has taken the form not only of Municipal and State Socialism, but of consumers' co-operation. This system has met with remarkable success within certain limits. Its value as a general solvent of the industrial problem is open to two criticisms: (1) Co-operation suffers from the reverse defect of Guild Socialism. It does nothing for the producer as such. The employee may no doubt be a member, though often he is debarred from being an official or a committee man. But hitherto employees have always been a small minority, whose interests were, therefore, unless protected by the custom, at the mercy of the goodwill of the rest, and even if co-operation so grew that the majority or even the whole of its members were also employed in production within the co-operative sys-

tem, it would not follow that producers as producers had their proper status. Every group of producers is a minority, and may neither secure the conditions nor the kind and degree of control in production which is their due. (2) Co-operation as a conscious movement started naturally with retail trade, works back to wholesale distribution, and thence again to certain forms of production, e.g. of boots, clothing, soap, and certain goods which directly serve the ultimate consumer. In other fields of industry co-operation has made no sensible mark, and it does not seem likely that it will do so without a fresh start. The question is whether such a start might not be given by the State. If the coal mines can neither revert to private enterprise, nor be worked from Whitehall, nor be committed to a Guild of Miners, the remaining possibility is that adumbrated in the Sankey Report. They might be entrusted to a body representing producers and consumers jointly. The producers would fall roughly into two sections, representing the manual workers and the management; and consumers into two sections, representing the interest of the householder and the industrial consumer, including the shipowner. It is possible that in such a constitution we may find a type which will fill the gap between the existing Distributive co-operation and the industries suited to State or Municipal management.

This solution is open to the objection that it is bipartite and may lead to a deadlock. What is to happen if the producers' and consumers' "sides" are in the end opposed, a position which has apparently brought some of the Whitley Councils to a standstill. An answer may be found in the division of the producers' side into the managerial, the technical and the operative. The interests of these sections are not identical, and in fact both the manager and the technician are more interested in efficiency and amount and quality of output than in conditions of employment. Hence for many purposes they would on the whole co-operate with the consumers' side. We may thus contemplate a tripartite division of the controlling body, one-third representing consumers, one-third the management and the technical staff, and one-third the mass of the workers. Contested questions would then be decided by a combination of two of these sections, and it would be probable that the consumers' view would have the advantage, but only when fortified by the more expert opinion of the management and technical staff on the one side, or by the human element of the operatives on the other.

The combination of producers and consumers in the directorate does not, however, afford a final settlement of the relations between them. Hitherto many of us have thought of the question too abstractly. Because the worker is a citizen we have thought in being governed by the State he is enjoying self-government, or because he is a co-operator we have thought it enough for him to be governed by a co-operative society. In reaction from this unreality the Guild Socialists proposed that the producer should govern himself, thereby, as we have seen, committing themselves to a sectional monopoly. We should keep clear on the point that self-government in industry means government by the collective organization of all concerned, and that consumers are concerned as well as producers. But in the government of an industry we should distinguish the actual direction of work which is a managerial function from the conditions under which the worker is to live, which the management must accept and not impose. How, then, are these conditions to be decided? Not one-sidedly, either by the management or by the workers, but judicially on behalf of the community by representatives of both parties with a jury or impartial element to decide between them. This is the Trade Board method[1] which I believe

[1] We are as a fact exploring two methods of impartial decision in industrial matters, one that of the Trade Board, the other that of the Industrial Court. The advantages of the Trade Board are (1) that it deals continuously with one and the same industry, so that the impartial element (those appointed members) become conversant with the technical questions of the trade and have a continuous responsibility for its well-being; (2) the bulk of the members of the Board are engaged in the trade and habitually settle questions by agreement. The appointed members act in the first instance as conciliators, and only fall back on their casting vote in the last resort. Even then from their position as a minority they have to gain the assent of one side or the other. The position is the nearest possible approach to a synthesis of self-government and judicial decision, and would therefore be in the closest touch with the self-government exercised by the managing council of the trade. On the other hand, a Central Trade Board is undoubtedly required to act as a final court of appeal, co-ordinating the decisions of individual Trade Boards and so in effect prescribing general standards of wages and hours.

The dual system of a Board of Management and a Trade Board for the settlement of disputes as to conditions, is in substance the plan to which the Government have been brought in the case of the railways and the suggestion is that we have here stumbled in characteristic fashion on a suitable model for general application. It makes no difference whether the "employers" are capitalists, co-operators or State or Municipal officials. The questions at stake and the methods of deciding them are the same.

INDUSTRIAL ORGANIZATION 215

to be no less essential to co-operative or State industry than to private industry. For neither the State, nor the Municipality, nor the Co-operative Society is impartial as between itself and its employees in questions of the organization of an industry. We have seen the Government trying to act both as executive, charged with the duty of getting the coal produced and the trains run, and as judge, deciding what it is just and reasonable for miners or railwaymen to receive. The functions are not compatible. The executive must separate itself from the judicial, and the State must have its own tribunals to decide, if need be, against its own executive, certainly to decide independently of the desires of the executive.

The key to an industrial solution is to be found in a division between the executive direction of industry and the impartial control, part legislative, part judicial, of the living conditions under which it is carried on. To this control belongs the regulation of wages, hours, conditions affecting health, and the status of the worker. Its general principles must be laid down by the State legislature, but it may be left to a Trade Board to adapt such principles to the particular needs of each trade. The question of the status of the worker and the right of dismissal cannot be left where it is. It will have to be determined probably by Trade courts forming for themselves, perhaps on the basis of resolutions of Trade Boards, a body of rules growing out of Trade custom. To give the worker some fixity of tenure consistently with the mobility required in a world of ever-shifting industrial requirements is perhaps the most difficult industrial question which has come within sight. It cannot usefully be discussed at this stage, but should be mentioned as one of the problems which can only be solved, if solved at all, by an organ of self-government, in which the balance between partners is held by an impartial element.

The industrial organization which we are thus led to contemplate is one in which unearned wealth would accrue to the community; the universal and elementary conditions of private work and remuneration would be laid down by law, and would be adjusted in detail, developed, expanded and improved as the conditions of each trade allow by Trade Boards; while industrial management would be in the hands of joint Boards of consumers and producers, the Municipality, co-operative associations, or private enterprise according to the nature of the industry, and the relative efficiency for varying purposes of which various forms of organization prove themselves capable. These are questions of the means wherein we are to be guided by experience of results, not questions of the ends by reference to which we judge the results themselves.

CHAPTER XI

DEMOCRACY

THE normal life of mankind is found, when we get below the surface, to be in a sense democratic. That is to say the life that men live together is a joint product to which the will, the passion, the intellect, the temperament of every one concerned makes its contribution.[1] I take this to be true even in a slave system. The slave takes his tone from the master, but no less fatally though much less consciously the master is the convex of the slave's concave.[2] The Assyrian conqueror on the *bas reliefs,* as Herbert Spencer was fond of pointing out, is himself inevitably tied to the rope by which he leads his prisoners. Our destiny is not our own temperament alone but that of all with whom we are associated. Each personality by a law that no doctrine of self-sacrifice can escape makes its own way whether by leaping rocks and piercing barriers, or by percolating like a lost stream through the sand; and each channel that it makes goes to determine the line of least resistance for its next neighbour. Perhaps the ultimate root of democratic principle is the

[1] The point has been well brought out by Mr. Ivor Brown in his work on *Democracy.*
[2] Still more markedly is the "mean white," a typical product of a system intended to degrade only the non-white.

conscious recognition of this underlying fact, with the deduction that if any are to be truly and morally free, all must be free. At any rate, equal freedom in a common life is the simple meaning of democracy. Where all nominal power is confined to one or to a few, or even to many, the development of the dominant section is no less distorted than that of the subordinate section. They are compelled to assert themselves, and at bottom, like Domitian in the recesses of his palace, they feel the terror they inspire. The sharing of government and responsibility alone inspires mutual confidence, hope and charity, the expansions of human nature as against its inhibitions.

The freedom of man in society, we have already seen, can never be absolute. It is always conditioned by the equal claims of others. It may be said to have two aspects. In the one, it is self-determination without mutual encroachment —a self-determination which holds not only for the individual, but for the class, the group, or generally any and every element of the community. In the other aspect it is the positive contribution of the individual (and again of every element of society) to the common life. In the second sense the common life is free when and in so far as each element is called on for its contribution, and no decision is taken till it has made itself heard and felt. This cannot mean that every man is to have his own way. Unless by a miracle of pre-established harmony, that would spell anarchy. It means that in some way each separate will is to be taken into account. How to secure this is the standing, and unsolved, problem of political democracy.

On paper the solution seems simple enough. Every one must have a voice and a vote. Before decisions are taken he is perfectly free to exert whatever influence he can. Once taken the decision is binding and he must obey. Minorities must give way and accept the view of the majority as the law of the sovereign democracy.

When we come to realities this solution proves very unsatisfactory. In the first place, it is not practically possible for every man to be consulted about everything. A handful of people acting together for a specific purpose, say the partners in a business, may so conduct their affairs; but the method is not applicable to large communities of high organization. Their government is a connected whole where one decision involves others in ways which even experts and those at the centre of affairs may not foresee. Popular intervention is necessarily intermittent, occasional, and very imperfectly instructed. The difficulties of democracy under this head are too well known to need detailed exposition here.[1] They are so great as to have suggested the view that in all high social organizations government, whatever its nominal form, is in reality government by experts. A score of heads of departments with able subordinates to help them govern the British Empire, it is thought, from Whitehall, while the press screams outside and every now and then succeeds in some "stunt" which disarranges the plans of the wise. Against this view has to be set that fundamental truth of democracy which has been indicated above. At bottom the British Empire runs it-

---

[1] Especially in view of the elaborate discussion in Lord Bryce's monumental work (*Modern Democracies, passim*).

self, not very much by voting power and parliamentary discussion, but simply because it consists of some 400 millions of living wills, each finding its own way in the world and so channelling the course of its neighbours. Out of these millions of interactions arise from time to time, now here and now there, situations calling for some organized action. It is here that the pundits of Whitehall make their appearance on the scene. They do not normally create a situation or a problem, but they find it and they experiment with a solution. Sometimes possibly the abler editor or the outside agitator finds the situation and propounds his ideas. But the point is that all this conscious intervention is secondary. It is the deliberate supervening upon the undeliberate and unconscious process which is the background and foundation of the social life. Now the democratic theory is simply that the propounded solution—the work if you will of the expert and the wise—should be referred back to the people whom it affects, whose unconscious or half-conscious actions have rendered it necessary, and who will have to adapt their lives to it. But it is here that difficulties really begin. Our analysis has shown that neither conscious democracy nor bureaucracy is really as powerful as it appears. It is, of course, easy for any one to do mischief; but the power of the most expert, upright and benevolent officials to order affairs well and improve the life of a community is narrowly limited to certain choices afforded by the turns which affairs themselves take under the impulsion of a myriad of wills. On the other side, the power of conscious democracy is practically limited to certain critical decisions, and largely to a veto on the proposals of the bureaucrat. These decisions detached in their utterance are concatenated in their effects in ways which even the expert finds it difficult to trace, and which are far beyond the grasp of any one who does not give his whole mind to social affairs. Hence, effective popular control is the fitful thing that we see, and must so remain unless or until it develops some organ superior to anything yet known. The difficulty of democracy is not so much that on which its older opponents insisted, the difficulty of a bad will or a selfish will—the difficulty is to get any will at all: that is to say, any stable attitude of mind laying down coherent principles which might be safely left to the expert to apply.[1] Instead of this, democracy is apt to bubble up into some emotional decision, and then relapse into a flat quiescence and leave everything to its rulers—until next time. As to an election, it is at best fought on some one or two of the thousand issues that come up during the life of a Parliament, and even so, politicians are so clever at confusing the issue, that when all is over the dispute can at once be resumed on the question what it was all about and what the great decision in fact decided.[2]

[1] On the conditions which justify us in attributing true "will" to any group and in particular to a nation, see McDougall, *The Group Mind,* esp. chaps. iii, iv and xi, which shows very clearly that collective will is not a mystical unity or metaphysical principle but an organization of individual wills of every degree of perfection and imperfection, varying according to positive and clearly specifiable conditions. The conditions militating against the formation of a true popular will are trenchantly exposed by Mr. Hobson in *Problems of a New World,* Part II, chap. viii.

[2] "Thus Free Government cannot but be, and has in reality always been an oligarchy within a democracy," but an oligarchy "not

Notwithstanding these difficulties, a majority decides, and a majority must decide. The rule of the majority is sometimes spoken of as a convention, but it is in fact inherent in government by discussion, whether the power be in the hands of the few or the many. In a council

in the historical sense of the Rule of a Class," but of guidance by the few possessed of special qualities and opportunities. The function of democracy is to prescribe the welfare of the whole community (as against that of any favoured section) as the End, to select those who are to find and apply the means, and to hold those selected to their duty—functions more easily fulfilled by negative than positive methods, by rejection and veto, than by initiation of policy. This substantially is Lord Bryce's final verdict (*Modern Democracies,* vol. ii, chap. lxxv). As we might put it, there is a "natural" oligarchy just as there is a "natural" democracy. The main direction of affairs, subject to the limits indicated, will always be in the hands of the relatively few who, having the capacity for handling them, are ready to use their capacity by giving sustained continuous attention to them. The average man, capacity apart, refuses this attention (Bryce, *passim;* cf. Hobson, loc. cit.). We might add that there is also a "natural" monarchy, not only in the sense that a Cæsar will force his way to the front, but in the deeper sense that men are always trying to invent Cæsars. They will have a figure-head within the dominant oligarchy to impersonate their cause and to give concreteness, concentration and living affection to their loyalty. By the use of the term "natural" I wish to imply that all these three tendencies persist even under institutions which ignore or seek positively to counteract them.

Contemporary criticism of democracy concentrates itself mainly on Representative Government as the nidus of oligarchy. Substitutes suggested are (1) the Guild system or Functional Government, which is discussed below; (2) Direct Government, by Referendum and Initiative. This is very fully examined by Lord Bryce, and on the whole with favourable results in the case of Switzerland. (In the case of America the evidence that he adduces seems, I confess, to warrant a more favourable verdict than his caution of three, two must have their way against one, and the only alternatives are the liberum veto, which is anarchy, or one-man rule, the advantages and disadvantages of which are a well-worn theme not to be further worn out here. Our object is to consider the bearing of majority rule upon the democratic principle. The first consideration is that it gravely emphasizes the drawbacks already mentioned. When there is so much difficulty in clearing an issue and arriving at a decision, it follows that a good deal of accident may go to the constitution of a majority. That a certain course commends itself to fifty-one per cent. of the population, gives it very little real authority over the course proposed by the remaining forty-nine per cent. Democracy would, in fact, be impossible if bare

will allow to pass.) But if direct government is to be effective either the problem must be comparatively simple, or there must be an exceptionally high development of popular intelligence and public spirit. (Lord Bryce, however, suggests that these are in fact markedly stimulated by the system, vol. ii, p. 477.) As far as present experience goes, however, the method appears quite inapplicable to the continuous work of government and legislation. It is possible to pick out certain big and intelligible issues for a popular decision where it would be impossible to obtain an intelligent vote on all the minor, and especially the technical matters, which constitute the bulk of legislation. So in administration certain big issues might be referred, and also big questions of personality. Indeed, a British General Election, like an American presidential contest, may be regarded as principally a referendum on the question whether A or B shall hold supreme power. (Lord Bryce shows conclusively that the attempt to make minor offices depend on popular choice utterly defeats itself through ignorance of the candidates.) It would seem, then, that the sphere of direct government in a great community is limited, but the future of democracy will depend largely on the power of using it well within these limits and perhaps on finding expedients for expanding them.

majorities ordinarily exerted all the power which they enjoy on paper. So far as this country is concerned, we have not, in fact, been so much troubled on this point as by the peculiarities of our electoral system which exaggerate the appearance of majorities. In geographical single-member constituencies, particularly on national issues, very nearly the same conditions repeat themselves over and over again. One constituency does not correct another, but there is a tendency for all to go the same way. Hence, the parliamentary majority of one side may be overwhelming, though in every consistency the other side commands a large minority. This produces an impression of a general trend of public opinion which overcomes the reluctance to use bare majority power. This particular defect might be removed by a better machinery, for example, by Proportional Representation. But with the best possible machinery majority rule needs to be exercised with a certain forbearance, which it is perhaps impossible to enforce by any positive institutions.[1] Majority decisions are necessary, and yet lack just that moral authority which democracy demands.

[1] The device of requiring a two-thirds (or larger) majority is sometimes wise—conspicuously so in relation to constitutional changes. But it also has its drawbacks. It is often quite as dangerous to withhold a positive decision as to conclude one prematurely, and the position of a country which has a majority but not the required majority for some necessary change, is not an enviable one. Not by the forms, but by the working realities of our constitution, this has been our case on the Irish question. It has been possible several times to obtain a majority for Irish freedom, but not such a majority as could force its way over obstructions. Meanwhile, the difficulties of the problem have grown with many years' delay.

Nevertheless, in a homogeneous population, the rule of the majority is tolerable, for the majority is not a fixed and definite entity. I am in the majority to-day on this question, and you are in the majority to-morrow on another question. It is turn and turn about, and every one must take the chances of the game. It is quite otherwise when a State is divided into two (or more) portions by race, religion, colour, nationality, or whatever it may be. In this case there may be a standing majority governing the community from its own point of view, and looked upon by the minority as an alien power. In such case it is a mockery to reply to the minority: "You, too, have the franchise; you are on equal terms with us. You live under a democracy; you govern yourselves; what more do you want?" The minority will reply: "We do not govern ourselves because we are not one with you. There is a spring of antagonism which dictates all your politics and saps the principle of community which underlies all differences in a genuine system of self-government. Your principle is at bottom oligarchic, for though you happen to be more numerous, yet you govern us on the fundamental principle of oligarchy, i.e. by the will of the governors without regard to that of the governed."

From this imaginary reply we can draw certain conclusions. The first is that Democracy implies in addition to Liberty and Equality a third or synthetic principle which we may call Community, which is difficult to formulate in precise terms and probably impossible to embody in any constitutional rule. A spirit rather than a formula, it means that all differences within the body which it animates are differences within and subordinate to a deeper and more comprehensive agreement, and that within this agreement no assignable section is left out. No body of opinion is ignored, because it is "only" the opinion of coloured people, or Germans, or Roman Catholics, or women, or casual labourers. More generally, though the desire of the majority is entitled to its due preference, there must be a sincere and constant effort to accommodate it to the desires of the minority. The aim is synthesis rather than victory.

A second conclusion is, that democracy in the sense of full equality of suffrage is not a sufficient answer to the claims of nationality. By nationality is meant the sense of forming a distinct community. Now, two distinct communities may form one state, provided that there is a fair give and take between them, and to be a permanency this must mean that at a deeper level they are also one community. This I take to be the history of the Anglo-Scot union. Both English and Scots have a distinct national sense, and if the English majority had habitually ignored, or over-ridden the Scotch, there would have been a Scotch separatist movement as vital as the Irish. But on the one hand, Scots and English were in all essential respects near enough to one another to feel a common unity as against the rest of the world; and on the other hand, the Scots have retained their own law, their distinctive institutions, and the tacit right to accept or reject new legislation for Scotland through their own representatives. Nor was there anything humiliating to Scotsmen in the circumstances of the union to put against its manifest commercial and political advantages.¹ The case shows the relativity of such a conception as nationality, and the wide possibilities of harmonizing it with other claims.

On the other hand, two communities like the British and Irish morally parted by long generations of oppression, rebellion, misunderstanding and mutual recrimination, cannot form a united working democracy. That the Irish can, if they choose, put 70 or 80 Sinn Fein members into the British House of Commons, is no answer to their demand to govern themselves. That is to say, democracy without community is not a sufficient solvent of nationality. This is not to say that the claims of nationality are absolute. No human claims are absolute till weighed against the counter-claims. The population that inhabits the town or piece of land that happens to be the commercial or strategical key to a great territory, has no indefeasible claim to a sovereignty which enables it to open or bar the door to a much greater population.² We may go further and deny that Czecho-Slovakia has any moral right to starve Vienna of coal.³ The rights of nationality depend on the possibility of a reasonable adjustment between the interests peculiar to a people and those which they share with others. This adjustment, however difficult to formulate in abstract and general terms, raises in fact precisely the same question as every

[1] Put more brutally, the Anglo-Scottish Union was based on a compact (commercial union) which was kept. The British-Irish Union was based on a compact (Catholic Emancipation) which for twenty-eight years was broken.

[2] See above, chap. ii, p. 43.

[3] Or Britain to profiteer in coal out of the necessities of a starving Europe.

other function of government. We have seen just the same difficulty in defining the liberty of the individual, and the principle of solution is the same.

The claims of a nationality inhabiting a defined and distinct territory can always be adjusted by internal autonomy, and an agreed basis for the management of common interests; and it is clear that they ought to be so adjusted. Permanent and marked minorities living intermixed with the governing majority, cannot be so treated. Nor is it only a question of permanent minorities. Any section of the community may be exposed by circumstances to the brunt of sufferings which it bears for the common good. The philosophical patience with which the rest of the community endures these sufferings is, at times, amazing. The stoicism with which our heroic non-combatants bore up against mud, trench-fever, and the hourly possibility of being blown to bits, was a feature of the national character which was for years the subject of daily self-congratulation. When in October of 1918 it became a question whether we should relieve the actual sufferers—our own sons and brothers, or enjoy a spectacular victory, there was no doubt as to the preference of popular emotion. It was all for more vicarious heroism. It realized to the full the remark of Aristotle that it may be fine to surrender the opportunity of a fine action to others, and it was in sum prepared for a further holocaust to our youth as food for its glory. To be short, the majority in a community may be as callous as you please to the sufferings of a minority. How are we to deal with this situation? It is true that it will not arise if there is that sense of community which we have seen to be essential to democracy. But if that sense is lacking, what are we to do? Try to cultivate it, no doubt. But in the meantime, are there any institutions which may assist its growth? In the particular case of nationality we have seen a possible solution in forms of autonomy adaptable to the variations of particular cases. This solution, however, depends on geography. When geography is of no avail, does any general solution remain? To avoid any exaggeration, we may put the matter in this way. For any workable democracy we may agree there must be *some* sense of community. Without it democracy simply will not live. It will break up into anarchy, faction, lynch law, terrorism, or some kind of tyranny—whether the tyrants be many or few. Let us then postulate a certain sense of community, but recognize that along with it there may be permanently or temporarily a feeling of what we may call "discommunity." Something like this we may consider to be the normal situation, even in a reasonably well-ordered State, and we have therefore to consider normal means of dealing with it. Let us first remark that the traditional theory of the sovereign state, particularly of the sovereign people, ignores the problem. For this theory, when the people has spoken that is law. What is worse, it is not only the Law, but also the Prophets. It has not only legal sanction, but moral authority. Every one on this principle is entitled to his voice and his vote; but when these are cast and the majority ascertained, the rights of the individual and the section surcease. One will must prevail. There must be decision. There must be organized, collective action.

Give all possible play to preliminary discussion, but expect and enforce eventual obedience.

In this theory, we must try to separate what is permanently valid from the elements due to historic causes. Historically, the theory of the sovereign state arose from the authoritarian conception of kingship, when the cosmic spiritual authority was removed. In the Middle Ages, government was barely distinguished from territorial ownership but conversely territorial ownership was based on allegiance and function, and behind and over all was a spiritual power, which was the ultimate judge of political right. With the rise of nations and the religious schism the king stood out as the tangible flesh and blood head of the State. There was none above him but God, and God was further off than Rome. In Protestant countries, he was the spiritual as well as the temporal Lord. From him the law hung as a chain from its support, and he himself was above it. True, there were limits, the old Estates or the budding Parliament; but these could either be regarded as his advisers, or incorporated with him as a definite body of persons who together constituted the recognizable sovereign. The essential was the conception of law and government, flowing from a superior, and that an ultimate superior possessing moral authority backed by physical force. Democratic theory in one form took over this conception with a single modification. The "sovereign" became servant; the people master. The whole was sovereign over the parts. The people knows no master, and is its own authority. This doctrine was always combated by an opposite theory to be found in different forms from

Paine and the American constitutionalists to Mill, according to which the individual only gives up to the State as much as is necessary to collective organization, and in the partition of territory, retains a private demesne for himself.[1] But with the rise of Socialism, this opinion became less popular with advanced thinkers. When schemes of reconstruction were on foot, personal liberty became a bore. And it must be admitted that the word was misused often enough to justify the apostrophe of Madame Roland.

In reality, the theory of sovereignty is rooted in conditions which are obsolete, and as applied to democracies involves confusion in ideas, and some consequent evils in practice.

(1) In a democratic community it is not true that there is any assignable person or body of persons who are recognized as exercising absolute power. In strictness, it is hardly true of any society; but the divergence from the truth increases with the growth and diffusion of popular intelligence and methods and habits of self-government. The "people" collectively can only exercise its power through some organ, and there is no organ which can unconditionally prescribe its will.[2] Lawyers may tell us that Parliament is omnipotent; but if Parliament began to do what they dislike, they would soon find legal principles to prove its limitations. Parliament

---

[1] It is an interesting point that Treitschke's early admiration for Mill led him to retain this conception, a qualification of his otherwise peculiarly harsh doctrine of the State.

[2] Unless it be the Referendum (see above p. 221, *note*). Even the authority of the direct popular vote, however, is limited by the considerations advanced lower down as to dissentient sections.

can legislate, but cannot secure that its legislation will take effect if it is opposed to the prevailing will, or to those social tendencies on which men act without deliberately choosing them. This is true not only of legislation affecting the country as a whole, and disliked throughout the country as a whole, but in large degree it is true of areas or sections in which there is a similar dislike. A single man may be helpless against the law, but when many connive, it is the law that is in the weaker position. Hence it is more and more clearly recognized that successful legislation must carry public opinion along with it. Nor is it only public opinion. There are limits to the power of the State over the single protestant. Hegel calls the State the absolute power on earth, but not all this power, with all its horses and all its men, could force a resolute conscientious objector to don khaki. Further, as the power of organization increases, sections of the people, e.g. trade unions, form independent conceptions of their interest, and the State is often forced to negotiate with them as equals. I do not for the moment inquire whether this is a good or bad thing. I merely note the fact, and I suggest that it is a natural consequence of the very same development out of which political democracy has arisen, and a very serious limitation on State sovereignty. If, in fact, we ask of our own country to-day not where legal sovereignty resides, but where the true power determining the acts of the community is to be found, I do not believe a single definite answer to be possible. The determining power is elusive: it is now here and now there. Often it is in the facts of the situation, rather than in any one will;

and it is a naïve kind of anthropomorphism which sees an intelligent will behind everything, attributing the rise of prices, for example, to the machinations of profiteers, and supposing that it could be stopped by a simple resolution to bring it to an end. I conclude that in any society, though there may be an assignable order of government to which obedience is habitually rendered, this obedience is not unconditional; the more democratic the society, the more definitely it is conditioned; and the factors really determining the life and behaviour of a society do not necessarily reside in this organ, nor are they capable of being limited by any specific determination which will hold good in all cases.

(2) The conception of a sovereign State implies the final authority of a politically organized community, and its independence of all other communities. This conception grew up in proportion as that of a higher authority covering all States grew weak. The result was a contrast between "the state of Nature" which Hobbes quite correctly saw realized in the international relations of his time and the state of law within each organized community. This fissure is morally wrong, and the source of war and world anarchy. It puts patriotism above humanity, and liberates political action from the moral law. The local divisions of mankind have their importance, and give rise to needs requiring the appropriate organs to satisfy them. But there are many relations—industrial, commercial, moral, religious, artistic, intellectual—which transcend all political boundaries, unite and divide men on quite other than political lines, and greatly need their appropriate organs of ex-

pression which should enjoy just as much respect as political government.

We have continually in preceeding chapters contrasted the individual with " the community," but we have never yet asked what community is meant. It has in fact, only been necessary hitherto to distinguish an individual and a communal principle, and what we have said would hold good as long as there were *some* community of which the individual is a recognized member, no matter what the community might be. The term, however, will no doubt have suggested to the reader the organized political community, i.e. the State. But this is not to be too hastily assumed. (1) To a Canadian does "the community" mean, say, the city of Winnipeg, the province of Manitoba, the Dominion of Canada, or the British Empire? On grounds of political organization any of these meanings might be justified, and in point of fact in current usage probably now one and now another of them would be understood according to the context. "The coal mines belong to the community." Good! but do the South Wales mines belong to South Wales, or to England? Do the English mines belong to England and the Scottish to Scotland, or all to the United Kingdom (including Ireland)? Or do they, perhaps, belong to none of these, but to humanity? To the patriot the last suggestion will seem a paradox, but the same patriot is by no means so clear that Persian oilfields belong exclusively to Persia, or Mexican oilfields to Mexico. We are quite prepared for the eloquent philosophy with which he will explain that these natural sources of wealth must be placed by those who happen to occupy the territory at the disposal of all mankind, and entrusted for that purpose to those who understand how to make use of them. But if that is so, have we a right to take advantage of a world shortage, to sell our coal abroad at "profiteering" prices; and if as a nation we have that right, can we deny to the South Wales miners the right to try to get back the profit in the form of excessive wages, on the ground that it is "their" coal? After all, the local view is not purely fantastic. The coal attracts a great population to work it. Should not at least a portion of its value be at the disposal of that population to reduce the disamenities of coal-mining?

In ethical truth, there is only one ultimate community, which is the human race. This community, alas! has never yet found organized expression.[1] To organize it is now the duty of statesmanship; but in the meantime the principle of community has been represented, with the imperfections and inconsistencies that we are observing, by organized bodies—States, Churches, associations of all kinds. When we speak of "the" community in any relation, e.g. as exercising a power or holding property we mean the community which is appropriate to the function that is in question. We are apt to think that the appropriateness is to be judged in the end by the joint operation of all the functions in the life of the State. That is not so. The functions of the State and its appropriateness as the organ which is to perform them are themselves to be judged in their relation to the life of humanity.

[1] The League of Nations, as at present organized and functioned, cannot be regarded as such an organ.

(3) The whole conception of sovereignty fuses two forms of constraint which it is the first duty of social philosophy to keep distinct—the constraint of power and the constraint of moral obligation. The medium of the fusion is the normal duty of obeying the law. Political organization is in general a condition of well-being, and our obligation to serve the general well-being carries with it, as a consequence, the duty of paying regard to the law. But political obligation is a secondary and derivative duty, and the supreme moral authority is not temporal but spiritual.

For this conception of a number of independent sovereign States claiming absolute allegiance and enforcing it by absolute power, we must therefore substitute a spiritual principle embracing all humanity, and finding organized expression imperfectly in various forms. Each such form has the value which belongs to a means, and the authority which legitimately attaches to an organization which is actually in being, and which we have no right to destroy or impede unless we are sure that it is doing positive harm, or at lowest that the same thing can be done, and done better, in another way. All these different functions require adjustment, and it is claimed for the State that the final word in adjustment is precisely its function. But this is not universally true, for the State has no means of adjusting, in the judicial fashion contemplated, its relation with other States; nor indeed, is it an adequate authority on any relations that transcend political frontiers. For supreme adjustment, we need a world-organization, the only ultimate physical authority comparable to the universal extension of the spiritual law. Nor, as we have seen, is the State an entirely trustworthy authority in relation to its own constituents, whose need of protection was the occasion of our embarking on this discussion.

Such considerations as these have suggested a functional theory of society. Social life rests on the combined operation of many activities. Any one of these which involves the work of many human beings should be organized, and become, primarily, self-governing. It would be a guild, and it will be clear that many of the guilds (e.g. coal-mining, or maritime transport) would be international. They are all in this view producers' guilds, and it is urged that the problem which we found so hard for State democracy of educating a real, instructed, and living public opinion, is solved by this method. For every coal-miner knows something about coal-mining, whereas he knows nothing about the government of the Punjaub. Ask him to vote on Indian administration, and he gives an unintelligent response, or no response at all. Ask him to vote on a method of winning coal or preventing an explosion, and he will not only give a judgment according to his knowledge, but will readily extend his knowledge and take a sympathetic interest in the methods of mining and the conditions of miners in Westphalia or Pennsylvania. Here then, it is suggested, we have the unit of democracy. Now, the various functions require co-ordinating, and for this we must have a Guild Congress, which will have, among other things, to lay down some of the general conditions under which any guild must work; and it seems to be suggested that the State should be placed on a level with other associations, having, like them, specific functions to perform, which must in turn conform to supreme conditions laid down by the representative gathering of all associations.

This view, which represents a theory that is still plastic and growing, rather than set and mature, has already been criticized from the economic side, where we concluded than the co-operative rather than the Guild organization was the true method of regulating economic functions. In political terms, however far we may go in distinguishing separate functions and giving them separate existence, we must never forget that a function is performed for the sake of some end whose interests our machinery must secure. The organization to which any function is to be assigned must include those specially interested in its performance, as well as the performers themselves. The government of a Church should represent the lay element, and the direction of education should not be left wholly to teachers.

On the other hand, there is a point to which in our economic analysis no special reference was made. The territorial divisions of mankind will remain, and will require the separate existence and authority of distinct "states." But most of the interests of mankind transcend state boundaries, and to give to such interests international organization is a sound element in the "Guild" idea. The miners of the world, the metal-workers, the textile operatives, the agriculturists, have their common interests. Trade Union as well as Capitalistic organizations have accordingly often sought international extension, and the Socialist ideal has always comprised an "International" representing all the manual workers of the world. There is an incipient internationalism in the co-operative movement. The Church of Rome still claims to be a world Church, and most religious bodies of any significance have their international ramifications. All this organization is rudimentary and imperfect as compared with the organization of States and of subordinate associations within each State. But among other things, they have the value of offering a cross-division of humanity which runs over all the boundaries of territorial isolation, and national antagonism. It is probably necessary to the effective union of humanity since we cannot overcome division—that it should be divided on different principles at the same time, so that men who are opposed in one relation find themselves co-operating in another. Moreover, if we could get the right basis for functional government in each case there is in every function something that appeals intimately to those peculiarly interested in it, and thereby calls out their public spirit and intelligence to better effect than the mixed and confused appeal of ordinary State Politics. In this relation, therefore, the Guild, suitably reconstituted, may have an important governmental function before it.

On the other hand, we must not depreciate the need of co-ordination between functions. We shall always require an organ of justice which sees fair between all organizations, all individuals, and we should add, between the individual and the functional organization. Now, this central function has in modern times been exercised well or ill, as the case may be, by the State. The main reason (apart from undemocratic government) why the

State has exercised it ill and become tyrannical, is its sovereign independence of other States, and the consequent need of defence and the fear of war. It is this which has tended to transform the modern State into a great hate-organization. Take this away and suppose the world one community, as slenderly organized, maybe, as the British Empire, but still with a general acceptance of certain common interests as essential to assured peace, and we then get the State as a peaceful association for the maintenance of internal justice. It is clear that the State could not grapple alone with international organizations. Their mutual relations and their several relations to States would have to be under the ultimate control of the World League, and it may be suggested—in view of what has been said of cross-division—that the World League should directly represent not merely States, but also international functions. However this may be, it is clear that if democracy is to succeed—or for that matter if civilization is to survive—the present aborted embryo called the League of Nations must develop in the direction of an International Federation. It is here, and not in the separate States, that the final adjustments must go forward. Thus, in a sense, it is here that sovereignty will reside. But the world State will not be sovereign as separate States have been sovereign, firstly because it has no foreign and potential enemy to arm it with the necessary claims to exert military discipline, partly because in the vastly complex whole men's allegiances will be subject to cross-divisions, being apportioned more in accordance with the true logic of feeling to the objects which really appeal to them and the organizations which have those objects for their centre. Patriotism, as the dying Edith Cavell foresaw, will regain its legitimate place as one loyalty among many to which human beings are called.

There are several ways in which State sovereignty must be limited by a World League from the outset, as is partly foreseen and provided in the existing covenant. The League ought to decide all inter-State questions, closely limit all armaments not only in the case of new members of the League, but in all countries, guarantee free commercial intercourse, assure certain elementary rights of individuals, and in particular serve as the court of reference between any State and recalcitrant nationalities. If England cannot settle the Irish question, the world should (and I fancy will) settle it for us. Subject to these limitations, the State will remain the organ of internal adjustment between the various organizations which are to carry on the main work of self-government. Nor do I think that the constituencies in the State Parliament would be either Guilds or co-operative societies or other functional associations. On the contrary, I think that here, too, it would be necessary to have a cross-classification as a counterpoise to powers of the associations which might too easily become excessive, and that we must seek a corrective to the obsolete geographical limitatons rather in proportional representation than in the occupational vote. It is the external problem, the fear of the foreigner, the false pride of Empire, the readily-aroused suspicion and hatred of those who cannot at once put their cases in the language of the people, that have in the main thwarted the working of democracy hitherto. The world, we have agreed, can only be organized in divisions, whether we divide by localities, or beliefs, or industries, or other functions. Now, however we divide sectional interests, corporate selfishness, jealousies, antagonisms, hatreds, make their appearance. In the world of to-day, the dangers of corporate selfishness within the State are not less than the dangers arising from the State itself. Functional organization has a great future, but subject always to adequate methods of co-ordination. I do not think the State will go far in the direct organization of industry. I think industries will organize themselves on a basis of co-operative self-government. But the relation between them and general conditions which all must observe, will be matters in each territory for the State organization to determine subject to certain supreme conditions laid down by the League of Nations.

The further discussion of these problems would take us from the field of Applied Ethics into that of Political Speculation. For social philosophy the firm conclusions are that the democratic community must be international; that in the whole every part—whether we divide by functions or localities—requires its own organ, has its own sphere of self-government, and its own right to maintain and enforce its views; that conversely there must be organs of adjustment maintaining the whole as a whole; that as a question of order, if it comes to physical force, the last word lies with the whole, or that which is its nearest and best representative; but that beneath all physical force there is a deeper spring of justice, and the ultimate supremacy rests with no organization whatever, but with the spiritual forces imperfectly apprehended in the minds of the wisest, and for that very reason legitimately appealed to, even by the humblest. Of all the retrograde movements threatening us, the most serious is the loss of grip on the hard-won conception of liberty—a loss typified in the prevailing belief that to fight Bolshevism it is necessary to kill Bolsheviks—and even cut off their supplies of chloroform for their hospitals. Perhaps the history of this adventure will teach the world once again that the spring of progress is spiritual, and that this spirit is not aided by the secular arm. Perhaps alternatively, a true spiritual authority will arise out of the present welter of half knowledge and conflicting dogmatisms; but it must be an authority true to its own spiritual principle, governing by the light of reason and through the convictions of men, indifferent to place and power, an organization, not of officials and monarchs, but of knowledge, wisdom and righteousness, the bodiless church of humanity in which the federated democracies of the world may find their soul.

INDEX

Ability, reward of, 161-165
Altruism, 10
Aristotle, 28, 101, 108, 117

Bentham, 5, 6, 10, 11, 19, 32, 61
Bequest, 192-194
Bryce, Viscount, 219, 222, 223
Bureaucracy, 209, 220

Capitalist system, 192
Character, 68
Coercion, 74-75, 86
Cole, Mr. G. H. D., 5
Collective achievement, 25, 128, 129
Collectivism, 22
Community, the, 22, 23, 38, 58, 64-65, 97, 188, 235
   sense of, 225-226, 229
Conscience, 77, 86, 92
Constraint, 48, 49, 50, 74, 77, 83, 84
Control of prices, 203, 204
Co-operation, 211
Custom, 27
Cynics, 101

Defectives, 157-158
Democracy, chap. ix
   direct, 222, 231
Desert, 107-113, 126, 138-141, 147
Desire, 12-13
Development, 18-19, 72, 75, 92-93, 126-127
   spiritual, 75, 133

Differentiation, 132
Dual control, in industry, 214
Duties, 35-36, 40-41, 44

Egoism, 10, 12
Endowment of motherhood, 160
Equality, chap. v; 8
   and inequality in historical development, 128-131
   proportionate, 107-108, 113, 114
Equity, 117
Ethics, 4, 5
   and politics, 4
Exchange, 149, 150
Expiation, 141, 144

Feeling, 8, 14, 19
Force, 98
Franchise, 97
Free institutions, 96
Freedom of contract, 79-80
Function, 124-125, 135, 190

Good, 14, 15, 16
   the common, 25, 30, 42, 43, 59, 70, 74, 91, 93, 98, 119, 122, 123, 128, 133, 141-142, 195
Government, 65, 95
   functional, 222, 237, 239, 241
   representative, 222
Green, T. H., 6, 30, 36, 41
Guild system, 210, 237, 238, 239

INDEX

Happiness, 6, 7, 8, 9, 10
Harmony, 14-20, 25, 35, 41, 43, 44, 50, 60, 74, 75, 92, 105, 120, 121, 122, 127, 128, 142, 147
Hegelian school, 31
Hereditary wealth, 191-195
Hobson, J. A., 41, 221, 222
Holland, Professor T. E., 36
Humanity, 242-243

Idealism, 4
Impulse, 17
Indecency, 81
Individual, 22, 87
Individualism, 22, 26
Industrial control, 186
Industrial Court, 214
Infallibility, 68, 93
Inheritance, 192

Justice, 104, 119, 134
and harmony, 171-172
communal, 148
commutative, 147, 167
corrective, 147
distributive, 125, 148
economic, 144
personal, chap. vi; 148
retributive, 141, 142, 147

Law, 27, 59, 115-118
League of Nations, 235, 240, 241, 242
Liberties, 64, 66, 79, 83-84, 90, 95
and law, 102-103
development of, 99-103
Liberty, moral, chap. iii
political and social, chap. iv

Living wage, 156-159
Locke, John, 29-30, 102

MacDougal, Professor W., 221
Majority rule, 222-225
Mechanism, 55
Mill, J. S., 7, 11
Mind, 99
Monotheism, 101
Moral law, 119-120
Municipal management, 208-209

Nationality, 43, 226-229
Nature, 28
law of, 29
state of, 30, 32
Needs, 112-113, 122-125, 152
Non-producers, 152-153

Obligation, 11-12, 31
Opinion, 68, 73

Personality, 36, 37, 38, 70, 71, 73, 74, 113, 114, 129
Pigou, Professor A. C., 156, 197
Plato, 28, 131
Pleasure, 9, 12, 13
Pleasure and pain, 8
Profit, 199, 201, 206, 207
Property, chap. viii
and liberty, 179, 182-184
and power, 181, 182, 183, 184
and responsibility, 180
common, 177, 192
limitations on, 175
private, 177, 188, 192
Prophets, the Hebrew, 131
Protestants, 102
Punishment, 126, 141-142, 144-147